The Guitar Man

SAM LI

Mark Eglinton &
Fiona Beattie

THE GUITAR MAN
SAM LI

Published in the UK in 2019 by Rudling House.

A CIP catalogue record for this book is available from the British Library.

ISBN 978-1-910957-03-5

Cover & Typeset by Jake Tynan

RudlingHouse

www.rudlinghouse.com

FOR SAM

CONTENTS

FOREWORD

It is over 50 years since I last saw Sam Li and yet my recollection of him is very clear - clear because he was clear and lucid. I was a struggling-to-survive guitarist who was working as a guitar salesman. The salesman's salary was principally through commission and, as such, we worked hard to sell at least one instrument a day. Of course, repairs and adjustments to guitars were done by Sam - the expert on guitars.

I met Sam shortly after joining the firm, in his tiny cubbyhole - for want of a better word - in the basement, and was immediately intrigued by him and the strangely peaceful atmosphere that surrounded him. He was the first oriental person I'd ever met and, being intrigued, I attempted to get to know him better.

I learned quickly that there was very little about guitars and their construction that Sam did not know. I also saw that he was also a very good guitar player, which intrigued me further.

Of course, being young and vain, I played guitar for him at the first chance I got, wishing to impress him, but Sam remained unimpressed although simultaneously encouraging. It was only a matter of time before Sam began recommending music to me to listen to and analyse.

The first group he recommended was the Four Freshmen. They were at their peak in the 1950s and their harmonies were very sophisticated. Shortly after, thanks to Sam, I discovered the music of Stan Kenton and, thereafter, I was on my way to further discoveries in Jazz music.

In ending this foreword, I confess I never knew if Sam was Chinese, or of some other nationality, but his demeanour was of a wise man and his help and guidance during the 18 months I saw him regularly are still with me today, even after over 50 years.

- John McLaughlin, 2017

INTRODUCTION

Sometime in 2016, I received an email from someone whose name I didn't recognise, asking if I'd be interested in exploring a potential biography of her late stepfather in collaboration with her. In my line of work, emails of this kind are not exactly uncommon and I open all of them out of sheer curiosity.

For author/biographers these emails are often the holy grail of new material. Fiona Beattie's message didn't say much other than to add that this man, Sam Li, wasn't just important to her but was also something of an underground legend in the world of guitar making and repairing in the 1960s and 1970s London music scene.

Interesting, I thought.

Then I did what anybody does first whenever they need more information: I Googled.

Nothing appeared whatsoever - at least not on the Internet's superficial surface layer. No Wikipedia page, no profile and certainly no images. In fact, there was very little Internet footprint to speak of.

On closer inspection though, while free-diving into the deeper layers of the various guitar magazine and manufacturer forums that exist, I saw Sam's name did start to crop up sporadically, often in passing, always in a hushed, revered tone and most commonly associated with work done on Peter Green of Fleetwood Mac's 1959 Les Paul, affectionately known as 'Greeny'.

In addition to this information which, in most mentions, resembled something of an urban myth, the research also led to other tangible mentions of Sam's career, not least an article about Slade's Dave Hill. Hill spoke most affectionately about Sam and a Sam Li custom-made Gibson-style guitar that he used during the bulk of Slade's most fertile years.

I thought: There's a great story here...

Unsurprisingly, most of the skeletal stories about Sam Li's life alluded to a man who, while occupying a position at the absolute epicentre of one of the wildest eras in the history of popular culture - the '60s and '70s' London music scene – was, by all accounts, something of a monosyllabic enigma.

With little in the way of fuss, Sam Li serviced these musicians with all their guitar needs, using fastidious attention to detail and passion. But he eschewed every other aspect of the loud and hedonistic lifestyle that they lived to the degree that he looked upon it with borderline disdain.

To that extent, it seemed that Sam Li's interaction with his clients was a culture clash in every sense but one that nevertheless fulfilled the needs of both parties for many years.

But to tell his story wasn't going to be easy, especially given the lack of information online and how secretive he clearly was about his life. Then a thought occurred to me: perhaps a person's personality - specifically a craftsman's - lives on beyond that person's life?

While guitars are by definition inanimate, maybe something of the maker's energy and spirit is retained within the wood, the headstock and the composition of the electrics.

In the specific case of the aforementioned 'Greeny' for example - a guitar we know Sam Li once held in his hands - it wouldn't be too much of a leap of faith to suggest that that theory appears to have been borne out over the decades. After all,

Metallica's Kirk Hammett, the guitar's current owner, previous owner Gary Moore and, of course, Peter Green himself, have all mentioned how this guitar seems not only to have a unique tone but also a personality entirely of its own. And that was just one instrument that Sam Li had touched.

In that, I felt I had the key to unlock this extraordinary man's life: the instruments he made and repaired and the people who played and still play them. I just had to find them so that a picture could be assembled.

Even so, the task of writing a traditional biography about a man who, even when living, didn't particularly want to be found, was never going to be straightforward. Some of the information on Internet forums was either conflicting or plain wrong, with the result being that I'd inevitably be led down some blind alleys to dead ends.

So be it, I thought.

I came to realise that - on a purely subversive level at least - failures to unearth information might actually be as significant to his story, as symbolic of how the man lived his life, as any of the times I might have struck biography gold.

And I was even prepared for the eventuality that I might never strike gold - that there just was no information to find. That too would have been fine (albeit not exactly great news for readers) and entirely in keeping with the life of Sam Li. With that acceptance at the forefront of my mind, I proceeded...

Perhaps not surprisingly, the act of 'finding' someone wasn't without its perplexities. Names were offered up; places, dates and conversations alluded to. Characters came onto the scene with vivid recollections to share, others ruled themselves out or simply didn't remember. Equally, conversations about various instruments purportedly made by or worked on by Sam sprang up from all over the world, with a variety of outcomes.

As quickly as new emails hinting at valuable information landed, previously promising potential leads went by the by. The process was an emotional roller coaster of hope and despair - the latter caused mostly by important potential interviewees who, for whatever reason, just refused to respond at all!

Of course, what I didn't realise, couldn't possibly realise until I had some distance between me and the writing, was that this was exactly what the story required: a search.

For every unanswered phone call, every case of mistaken identity ("Sorry, I thought you meant Stan Lee..."), every one-line scrap of recall about a fleeting encounter with Sam sometime in 1970, I was slowly but surely forming a picture. Even the nothingness added something to that picture. Meanwhile, I was becoming a little emotionally attached to this man whose sole photograph stared implacably back at me from the wall beside my computer screen.

Whatever happened, I was getting to know Sam Li on some level,   an act that for some reason I felt the man himself would have possibly found quite repellent. Whether anyone else would get to know him was dependant entirely on what came to the surface.

CHAPTER ONE

It was the cold winter evening of February 24th 2005. Sam Li's life story had reached its final chapter. The heart monitor in the intensive care ward that checked his vitals was showing very low readings while a kidney machine was barely keeping Sam Li alive. That he knew little of his perilous predicament was perhaps a blessing. He was in a coma.

The ICU was at full capacity that night - with the hospital struggling to keep an outbreak of the superbug Acinetobacter under control. Sam Li had initially been admitted because of an aneurism. He was making a good fist of surviving it. But ironically it was the secondary superbug that was now posing the graver threat to his life.

As time passed, the family discussed who would leave and who would stay. His stepdaughter, Fiona, decided that she would stay with Sam as she didn't want him to be left alone in such a stricken state.

Fiona and her partner, David, departed Sam's room for a coffee break while leaving specific instructions that they should be called if anything about his condition should change. Within a matter of seconds, a nurse came running down the corridor, asking them to return immediately.

'He didn't want you to leave,' she explained.

As Sam clung to the threads of life, Fiona and the nurse chatted like friends for the remainder of that late evening. The conversation spanned many subjects - not least Sam's career in the music business and his lifelong love of jazz. They even put one of his favourite jazz songs on as background music - perhaps as comfort, or maybe in an effort to keep him in this world. As the music gently played, with his dark hair and his face unspoiled by lines, Sam Li's youthful appearance, even while unconscious, belied his advanced years.

'I can't believe he's seventy-seven...' the nurse said.

At 2 a.m., Fiona curled up exhausted on the sofa outside Sam's room. An hour or so later, she was awoken by the commotion of a doctor bursting into the room. The news was bad. Sam's kidneys were failing. His vitals were dropping away.

'He's going,' the nurse sighed, 'but he waited for you.'

After a few minutes, Sam Li's breaths became shallower still. The monitor signalled nothing. It appeared as if he'd gone.

And then the breaths came back, faintly, but just there.

'He's holding on,' the nurse confirmed. 'He doesn't want to go.'

But it was his time.

'Your mother is waiting for you,' Fiona whispered in her step-father's ear.

And with that Sam Li departed this Earth.

That night, snow had fallen. Her sister, Sam's daughter and her partner – who'd come to see Sam for the last time - drove Fiona home. It was 8 a.m., and the sun was just rising. All around, the landscape was turning white - a delicate, untouched blanket of snow was forming and leafless winter trees stood silhouetted against a skyline where a large, pink disc was appearing behind the 19th century church in Dulwich. On the morning of Sam Li's passing, the earth could not have been more picturesque, beautiful or peaceful.

Moments from - and reminders of - her stepfather's life, and her involvement in it, replayed through Fiona's mind

2

on her way home: the vinyl collection Sam had kept - with the records given to him by clients unopened and still in cellophane wrappers; the daily diet of music; the nonchalant talk of session musicians and the phone messages left requiring Sam's attention - 'Please ring Alice Cooper's roadie' or 'Please ask Sam to call André Previn's secretary back,' or 'A bottle of champagne from Labi Siffre was delivered earlier...'

Fiona reminisced more generally about growing up in a vibrant household where music played constantly - with her mother, Babs, playing piano, her brother, Frazer, playing percussion on whatever objects came to hand and Sam playing his jazz guitar. In every room there was either a radio or a record player. She smiled at the thought that Sam Li loved music as much as he loved life. To him, they were one.

However, Sam Li's years were inevitably as finite as the number of musical notes that can be played. And, in the same way as Sam often said that musicians would run out of melodies eventually, he himself had run out of time on this Earth.

True to form, Sam Li had arranged his own funeral several years prior to his death. Ever the perfectionist, any man who routinely vacuumed his jacket each morning could not possibly have left that onerous task to someone else.

Furthermore, the man who spent his latter life dressed in the very best suits had also made sure that, in death, his casket was the most expensive type available. He had clearly felt that he would not be able to rest easy until all this had been done.

On March 3rd, the family gathered in Sam's flat in Bayswater to await the funeral hearse. It arrived on time and parked outside. The church was only a few minutes away up the nearby hill. As the assembled group prepared to start walking behind the hearse, an embarrassed funeral director quietly said, 'I'm afraid there is a problem. The hearse has broken down.'

The group was stunned. The director explained that as the casket was so heavy it couldn't be carried. He asked if it would be acceptable to use a trolley.

Never in a million years! Fiona thought to herself. Sam would never have tolerated that.

Thereafter, Sam Li's funeral descended into a catalogue of unfortunate errors that might just have amused the man himself. The service ran late; everything that could have gone wrong went wrong. As the family gathered the next day to reflect on the man's life, nobody could ignore the irony of how the perfectionist's funeral had played out less than perfectly. Perhaps from beyond the grave Sam Li was having the last laugh after all. Maybe somehow he had sabotaged his own funeral!

CHAPTER TWO

'Macaw ask parrot if mango ripe, he say one, one'

(You should not tell everything. Room should be left to others to find out some things for themselves.)

Sam Li was a man of many secrets. Some of them remain so, particularly in relation to his early life. You could say that he contributed to his own mystique. As he navigated life, he neither kept much by way of mementos, nor did he discuss many aspects of his upbringing. 'He just wasn't a man of words,' his stepdaughter Fiona says. 'His deeds spoke so much more loudly.' Whether this was intentional or not is anyone's guess. Sam Li only left us his work.

From all accounts this reticent air wasn't in any way indicative of his broader personality. Indeed, Sam Li had his own unique ways of exhibiting great kindness and care to those that he loved. 'He was a thinker, a worrier and very sensitive, and I didn't ever hear him say a bad word about anyone.' Fiona recalls. 'If he did think something badly of someone, you never knew it and would never hear about it.'

What is known is that, following his birth in Georgetown, Guiana, on January 5th 1928, there was a mix-up with the specifics of his birth registration. Instead of being registered as Frederick Lew-a-Loy - the family name - his name was somehow registered as simply Samuel Li.

His mother, Rosalind, and father, Benjamin, from Indonesia and China respectively, had seemingly met in Suriname at some point in the mid 1920s. They had subsequently made their way to British Guiana to live although they'd returned to Suriname sometime afterwards for their son's baptism ceremony.

To the best of anyone's knowledge, his mother never worked and his father had some kind of business in Georgetown. Sam had an elder brother, Joe, and three sisters, Mary, Joyce and Dolly. From all accounts it was a simple, family-orientated life lived in a house in the seaside suburb of Alberttown, a house that was often full of friends and relatives. To everyone in Guiana, he was known not as Sam, but as Sonny Li.

What is not known is the exact nature of this young man's life while growing up in Guiana, except a childhood love of music and an interest in detailed craftsmanship. Perhaps that's no surprise given that Sam's elder brother, Joe, with whom he was seemingly very close, was reputedly a joiner of considerable ability who taught his younger brother the fundamentals of woodworking at a young age.

Likewise, mentions of a close friendship with members of a Quail family kept surfacing (more of them later), as did references to another close friend called Dick.

Edmond Leu (childhood friend): *As youngsters, Sam and Dick could chat all day. They'd go out for the whole day, ride home and then continue talking outside Dick's parents' house - a huge house on three storeys. They'd stand at the gates talking until 8 p.m. when Dick's mother would come out and say, 'Oh boys, leave something back for tomorrow.'*

Beyond his broad friendships, specific details of Sam's abilities at school or elsewhere later are thin on the ground to

6

say the least. But it seems that he too became a joiner/cabinet-maker while in Guiana - and he was seemingly one with a fussy, fastidious attention to detail that would stand him in good stead. From all reports he continued in this trade throughout his twenties - making and perhaps selling fine handmade furniture - while also playing social music with friends.

At some point he also married and had a family, but the private nature of his immediate close circle has prevented much else in the way of detail from coming to light. Indeed, some general research into Guianese culture has confirmed that, on the whole, privacy and respectfulness sit at the forefront of family values.

Jewel (Sam Li's eldest daughter): *Everyone called him Sonny. He was always known as Uncle Sonny in his hometown. Sam was a name that he took in England only. My grandmother raised me in a fairly conservative home. She seemingly liked Sonny very much. The subject of Sonny in general is a bit of a sensitive one, however. Regarding specifics, I can only really relate what I've been told by elders. I spent a good proportion of my young life hoping one day to see him. I wanted him in my life again. It was always on my mind. But you have to understand that topics like parental issues were never really discussed - even though I constantly asked questions. What I do know is that my father left Guiana when I was very young. I recall that when I started kindergarten, he wasn't there.*

Worth considering perhaps is the fact that British Guiana, the country of Sam Li's birth, has had an undeniably complex history.

Having been initially settled by the Dutch in the early 17th century, three colonies, Demerara, Essequibo and Berbice were then taken over by the British in 1796 following hostilities with the French who had, in turn, occupied the Netherlands. Throughout the nineteenth century various to and fros occurred until, in 1831, the three colonies merged to become one united colony entitled British Guiana.

Initially, British Guiana's economy was entirely founded on sugar production, until cane prices collapsed in the late 19th century. Diversification inevitably followed - with rice farming, forestry and later, mining all becoming important contributors to the colony's income.

During the early part of the twentieth century, the socio-political fabric started to change. Britain imposed a series of constitutional changes on the colony that weren't popular. This culminated in a state of emergency being declared, followed by military occupation in 1953 as the fear of a rise in Communist ideology sent shock waves back to London. For the next four years, under the direction of the British Colonial Office, British Guiana was under the direct control of its British Governor.

Life for young people in Guiana, perhaps understandably, must have seemed to be without opportunity. Jobs were scarce. The wider world called loudly.

At some point during the late 1950s, Sam Li must have decided that he himself wanted a better life and, to achieve that, he enrolled in the Windrush Programme – a scheme whereby the Empire Windrush cruise liner initially facilitated the transport of men from the Caribbean to the UK where, in turn, they would be allowed to settle and work as UK citizens under rules laid out by the British Nationality Act of 1948.

When the Windrush first anchored at Tilbury Docks, Essex on June 21st 1948, its arrival was symbolic as the starting point of a wave of Caribbean immigration. Half a million people entered the UK under these rules between 1948 and 1971. Many of them (there were inevitably stowaways) paid £28 - the equivalent of £1000 in today's money - to travel and their presence was vital for a country whose labour force had been weakened markedly in the aftermath of World War II.

On board on each trip were people with a vast range of skills and attributes. Mechanics, clerks, engineers, cabinet-makers, welders and domestic workers were the most frequently given occupations on the application but, on one of the first voyages, there was also a retired judge, a potter, two actresses, three boxers and two piano repairers.

Men outnumbered women three to one and there were also many children on board. The most popular destination was London. Those who initially had nowhere to stay were housed in a former air raid shelter close to Clapham South underground station with the result being that Caribbean communities soon developed in the Brixton and Clapham areas. Others planned to go to Liverpool, Birmingham, Manchester and Plymouth.

In recent years, of course, these immigrants have become known as The Windrush Generation and their (and that of their subsequent offspring's) precise immigration status became something of a national scandal. Individuals were detained, denied legal rights and, in some cases, faced with deportation - despite having lived, worked and generally contributed to British society for decades.

After a leaked report that caused much outcry, apologies were issued by the Home Office, compensation was offered (not yet implemented in some instances) and future fees waived for those affected. Meanwhile, as recently as August 2018, it was revealed that many members of the Windrush Generation were still living in an essentially destitute state while awaiting a decision on their status - people with jobs, homes and, in some cases, children.

Sam Li was one of the individuals who arrived in the UK from the Caribbean (or from any other Commonwealth country) prior to 1971 and, when he did so, the understanding would have been that he was entitled to permanent leave to remain in the UK provided he didn't depart for a period of more than two years. By the late 1950s, immigrants were travelling to the UK by aircraft rather than by cruise ship.

Given that this was an automatic right at the time, in many cases no documentary evidence was either given to, or requested from, members of the Windrush Generation for the four decades that followed their arrival.

In 1959, Sam Li would obviously have had no idea how divisive the Windrush Programme would later become. At the time, for him and for many other UK immigrants, it was simply a means to an end - a pathway to a potentially better quality of life in a country many miles from home but one that had, at least, some governmental connection to his homeland. But more than that, for Sam Li specifically, a move to the UK in 1959 made complete sense from a couple of perspectives.

Firstly, many of his friends and associates had similar ambitions. Guiana, sadly, offered little in the way of opportunity for young men like him beyond the country's traditional, moderately paid jobs. There was, therefore, a distinct ceiling of achievement in place for young people. And that ceiling - relative to the possibilities that a bustling city like 1950s London might offer - was undeniably low.

Furthermore, by 1959, thirty one year old Sam Li had already been engaged in work as a merchant seaman for some time - making regular voyages from Georgetown that lasted many weeks or even months. As much as this represented relatively stable work that prepared him in some way for the realities of being away from Guiana for long periods of time, there's no

10

doubt that he wanted even more.

Secondly, Sam's family life was at what could best be described as a transitional stage. His first marriage had broken down. By this point he was either divorced or at the very least separated from his wife, who remained the primary legal caregiver for their daughter, Jewel. Also, both of his own parents had passed away.

In every sense, Sam Li's life was at a crucial crossroads. Here was a man from simple roots who loved friends, family and the joy of playing and listening to music. But here too was a man who envisaged so much more for his life than his homeland could possibly offer. Perhaps the moment had arrived for Sam Li to test what the wider world might offer him?

A decision was clearly made - one that surely wasn't taken lightly with a family and young daughter in the equation. Nevertheless, in 1959, Sam made a leap of faith that would completely alter the direction of his life. He boarded a BOAC flight and left the West Indies behind.

A day later, he arrived in London with little in the way of possessions and soon found himself a place to live in a small apartment in Princes Square, Bayswater. One item that did make the trip across the Atlantic with Sam was his jazz guitar.

Dick Cheung and Iggy Quail were two Guianese friends, both of whom had travelled over to England. Sam and Iggy had had previous musical dealings. Together they'd been in a jazz band back home in Guiana. Iggy was a gifted pianist; Sam Li loved nothing more than to play jazz guitar as accompaniment. Rumour has it that Sam and Iggy, flushed with the excitement of being in such a buoyant music scene, reformed their band from their homeland in those first few weeks together in London. Another suggested that Sam played at one time with legendary bandleader Jack Parnell. It may well have happened. Photographs

11

exist of the two men together.

Although Sam Li could not have known it at the time, his alliance with Iggy Quail meant he was already in exalted musical company. In the years after hanging out with Sam, Iggy would become something of a London jazz legend. He retained that status until his death in 2000 at the age of 74.

As a pianist in a trio that mostly frequented Soho's underground jazz circuit in the early 1960s, Quail became something of an influencer in the London music world.

Later, Iggy's association with Jamaican 'Cuddly' Dudley Heslop led him to form a band called the Dominoes, who were heavily influenced by early rock 'n roll. In the '70s, his stock rose further. Iggy Quail hosted jazz all-comers sessions, initially at The Stapleton in Finsbury Park and later at Dingwall's in Camden Lock, where he shared the stage with literally hundreds of musicians over many years in residency.

Another Guianese friend, Edmond Leu, was in the RAF and met Sam via Guianese friends in London. He travelled back to the Bayswater flat on the weekends regularly to visit his friend.

Edmond Leu: *I knew that, before Sam came to England, he was a joiner back in Guiana. And this was in a time when joiners had to be very, very good. I also know that he played in a band with Iggy Quail. Iggy's family had an optician business. They played music for a local radio station in Georgetown called ZFY.*

By early 1960, Sam's daily life at that time entirely revolved around the Bayswater part of London and, significantly, its jazz scene. Above and beyond everything else, Sam Li loved notes, scales and melody - everything that combined to make music so limitlessly discoverable and exciting.

Fortunately, Sam Li's timing was perfect. London, especially Soho, was the epicentre of a thriving jazz scene that had been steadily growing in the aftermath of the relaxation of Musician's Union regulations that prevented American musicians travelling to the UK to record and play music.

Louis Armstrong's visit to London in 1955 was the beginning of a jazz explosion. This, in combination with the influx of African immigrants and people from other Commonwealth countries who arrived on the Windrush Programme, made the diversity of London's music scene complete.

By the time Sam Li arrived in London, a jazz scene that included a whole host of musicians from the Caribbean was already established. All he had to do was allow himself to be absorbed into it all.

And that he did.

On Friday nights, the Prince Alfred pub on the corner of Queensway and Porchester Gardens was undoubtedly the happening place to be locally. In the Prince Alfred pub, there was a weekly audience of players and listeners alike. Shirley Bassey (who reputedly lived in the flat below Sam's), socialite/model Christine Keeler and jazz singer Lucky Gordon were regular attendees.

A little further afield, Soho was the place for late night jazz. At the centre of it all in the early 1960s was the Sunset Club on Carnaby Street - which remained open, ironically, until sunrise and beyond. Run primarily for and by the black community, this club allowed the locals to mix with American GIs while Caribbean and Latin American-influenced music flourished - all played to such a high standard and with sufficient style that seemingly made the local musicians envious.

Elsewhere there were other jazz hotspots. The Flamingo Club on Wardour Street, which would later become synonymous with Mod culture, was one of the first jazz clubs to play music with amplification. Again, it was a place with broad cultural reach where Caribbean sat comfortably with British rhythm and blues. Other notable clubs where jazz was played were Club '59, Club '77 and, of course, the famous Ronnie Scott's, first located in Gerrard Street and later at 47 Frith Street.

On other days and nights, it was Sam's own flat that resounded to the sound of music and laughter. He just loved to play Cuban and Brazilian sounds while his friends sat around talking music in a smoke-filled room. It was as if a small part of Guiana had been lifted up and transported to London. And this, given the commonly accepted nature of the country's people, was no bad thing.

Because of both their history and the enduringly challenging nature of their environment, it's as if Guianese people have been conditioned to deal with adversity on a daily basis. Inhospitable weather, unpredictable sanitation, unpleasant insects and power cuts are a matter of daily routine in Georgetown. The population merely roll with the punches day-to-day.

In post-war Britain, there were no doubt challenges to face - not least those related to finding work and accommodation so far from home in a country where signs were shockingly known to read 'No blacks, no Irish, no dogs.'

Regardless, as inhospitable as Britain may have appeared, these challenges were arguably still less than those faced in the Guianese people's homeland, where political uncertainty was part of daily routine. In addition, Guianese people tended to smile through adversity and so it's no surprise that the community that was already established when Sam Li arrived in 1959 welcomed him with open arms. In return, Sam Li would always remain resolutely proud of his homeland and its cultures.

There's an old saying in Guiana: 'hand wash hand, make hand clean.' Fundamentally speaking, Guianese culture embodies kindness to others and passion above anything else. It's normal for cooking to be shared, even by those who have least to offer. That's just how Guianese people have always been, and that's still the case today with those who live in England but consider Guiana to be their true home. Despite the fact he lived in the UK for the majority of his life, it's likely that Guiana would always have occupied a place in Sam Li's heart.

David (Sam Li's nephew): *I knew Sam from back in Guiana in the early '50s, but, because he was working away on the ships so much latterly, I rarely saw him. In 1960, I decided to move to England to be with my dad who was already working here in Chinatown.*

So, on the 9th of May 1960 I arrived at Gatwick Airport. All I had on me along with my passport was a picture of Sam. All he had was a picture of me. That's how we found each other! I stayed at Sam's for a couple of months and then I moved out to start studying and working. I think he started working in the music shop shortly after I left, but it's a long time ago.

Sam Li was living the life of a musician in a time when London was populated with pockets of different scenes, many of them underground. Fittingly, on his passport at the time, his given profession was listed as 'musician'.

Inevitably, playing guitar as often as he did led Sam to establish a reliable source of guitar consumables - strings, machine heads, bridge-pins and such. Inevitably too, much like anyone in London at the time who was looking for the best in service and accessories, this desire led Sam Li directly to the door of Selmer Musical Instruments Ltd.

No recounting of the story of Selmer would be complete without mention of a man by the name of Ben Davis. Having left the British Army in the aftermath of World War I, Davis taught himself to play the saxophone out of a fascination with the sound of Dixieland and jazz – both of which were becoming popular in England at the time. Soon, he became proficient enough to play with big bands, including one of his own, and he would also write a book about the instrument entitled, simply, The Saxophone - published first in 1932.

Selmer was originally a French-owned company founded by Henri Selmer on the outskirts of Paris. It was Ben Davis who had the foresight to establish the Selmer company identity in England - initially in first floor premises at 126 Charing Cross Road in London.

By 1932, on the back of considerable growth, Selmer outgrew their first site in London and relocated to a new base at 114-116 Charing Cross Road. From here, the company expanded rapidly in both scale and reputation. By 1939, Selmer was arguably the UK musical instrument industry's biggest company.

By the 1950s, Selmer's sphere of influence was split equally between manufacture and retail. Amplification products and, later, organs were built at a factory on the first floor of a building on Theobald Road, Holborn, located behind the public library.

After initially importing RSA equipment from the United States (RSA was a company purchased by Selmer who themselves had produced amplifiers under the RSA and Truvoice names), Selmer started manufacturing their own guitar amplifiers under the company name, with the TV15 and TV6 being the most popular early designations.

By 1960, of all the music stores in London's West End at the time, Selmer Musical Instruments Ltd had by far the most glowing worldwide reputation, with ornate bronze columns framing a multitude of the best that Gibson and Fender had to offer at the time. Where some of its local competitors thrived on a kind of workmanlike charm, Selmer oozed class at shop floor and office level. Every item for sale carried a bespoke price tag; every salesman carried a smile and the expertise to match it.

Doug Ellis: *I joined when I was just nineteen as a shop assistant. I begged the boss for a job as I remember. I was such a pain in the neck. And I also seem to recall that we had to wear a shirt and tie – which was in keeping with the overall look of the place.*

Ben Davis and his brother Lou owned the whole building and, from memory, the ground floor was the showroom. Upstairs, I think, was an organ showroom. Above that there were another couple of floors - one was accounts and the other was perhaps the typing and hire purchase departments.

The front of the shop was very polished - lots of plush glass showcases with beautiful, gleaming instruments inside. There was an accordion player called Phil who had a real gift for creating displays.

Selmer sold everything apart from pianos: organs - particularly Lowry organs, saxophones, trombones and some stringed orchestral instruments but not very much.

The guitar department was fenced off a bit behind a glass window at the back, partly because it was fairly noisy because we had amplifiers. There was a Formica top running round the counter to a desk in the corner and there were obviously guitars hanging on hooks on the wall. In those days there were two-pin electrical sockets - all highly dangerous - with amplifiers underneath!

As attractive as the shop floor was, the floor beneath had another atmosphere altogether. The basement was where the repair work was carried out. This was the hallowed domain of the set-up guys. Here, hidden from the pristine world above, specialists in all manner of musical instruments operated from a series of workshops along this narrow basement corridor.

A technician by the name of Dick Clifford, in conjunction with salesman extraordinaire Jerry Donahue, reputedly made numerous key design improvements to Fender's Stratocaster and Telecaster guitars in these early Selmer days. Donahue, although an American by birth, would later become a pivotal figure in the British folk music scene courtesy of his work in Fairport Convention and Fotheringay.

Elsewhere in the basement, in the cluttered closet-like workshop next door, an extravert Italian man, Nando Fabi, reputedly sat completely immersed in accordions and their associated components.

Then there were Laurie and Albert - the brass guys - single-handedly keeping the London '60s big band sound going, all from a room no bigger than the average telephone box.

Doug Ellis: *The basement was an absolute tip. It was a riot down there. There was a canteen at one end, a whole bundle of defective amplifiers that didn't work, Dick Clifton's workshop and, beside that, Nando Fabi's workshop.*

Nando – who would later become very successful when setting up his own company called Elka-Orla, a distributer of Italian organs and accordions – would come in every morning and slap everybody hard between the shoulder blades while singing in Italian. He called Dick Dickamino and he couldn't pronounce Doug or Dougie so he called me Doggie, onto which he added something adjectival like Doggie, my besta pal.

So *he'd get into his workshop and start singing about Dickamino at the top of his voice. Dick, a quiet, single man who enjoyed square dancing in his spare time, would start singing back to him – usually something about the Italian war record. I don't think Dick, who was quiet and reserved, particularly liked how loud he was. They had a love/hate relationship.*

In another room, there were two people called Laurie and Albert. They were an institution; there wasn't much they couldn't do with brass instruments. They kept themselves absolutely to themselves to the extent that they'd just sit there all day repairing, talking to each other quietly, and then they'd go home. They didn't join in with anyone else at all. They were just Laurie and Albert!

John McLaughlin: *Dick was a really nice guy who worked with Sam. He had a nice sense of humour also. I'll never forget one joke he told me – referring to all American money on which is written: 'In God we Trust.' 'Yes,' Dick said, 'others pay cash!'.*

Dick knew guitars like the back of his hand – an excellent luthier...

To support phenomenal 'Swinging Sixties' driven sales volumes, the Selmer repair and support staff obviously had to really be geared up to their respective tasks. Jobs came in fast, and they had to go out even faster. Repairs and 'setups' (the initial tuning and calibration of a newly bought instrument) were at an all-time high as a result of this gathering boom. Consequently, Selmer only hired the very best people because they relied on their reputation as being peerless in every aspect of the instrument business.

Already a man of exacting standards, as illustrated by his detailed cabinet-making work years prior, Sam Li felt the same about using the very best regarding accessories for his own guitar. Consequently, as time passed, the affable - and clearly knowledgeable - Sam became well-known to the Selmer's staff as a man who possessed great taste and also one who insisted on fastidious attention to detail.

Jewel (Sam's daughter): *I've heard over the years that he had specialised in very detailed cabinets before he left for England. He was seemingly making very specialised pieces and I'm told that the build and varnishing was very high quality.*

Sooner or later, as conversations became longer on each trip across town for hardware, it seemed inevitable that there might be a meeting of minds whereby Selmer might ask Sam Li if he wanted a full-time position in guitar setup.

After all, to everyone involved, it surely made total sense. Sam needed a regular income to support his musical endeavours. Equally, Selmer could certainly welcome his considerable knowledge. In late 1960, those two worlds collided. Sam Li became Selmer's new guitar setup and repair guy after being appointed by the manager. And this was only the beginning...

Doug Ellis: *We were fortunate enough to have a wonderful manager in those days - a man by the name of Jack Moore. He was a funny little bloke, about whom I could relate quite a few stories, but he was very good to us and I liked him enormously.*

CHAPTER THREE

Sam Li settled quickly into life in Selmer's basement. The setup jobs and repairs came quickly and were turned around equally so. After all, the music business was expanding fast as a sixties scene took hold. Musicians were playing gigs around town and needed functioning instruments to do so. It would be no exaggeration to say that Selmer was the focal point of everything that was happening in London related to musical instruments in the early 1960s. Musicians shopped there; aspiring musicians worked there to make ends meet.

Doug Ellis: *Everyone came into Selmer. I saw Jimi Hendrix in there - The Beatles also on more than one occasion and Tony Hicks from The Hollies. It was all normal and very exciting. Saturdays were particularly frenetic. Nobody ever got the day off and you'd never be able to take a lunch break. Somebody would be sent out to fetch sandwiches for everyone. A Daily Mirror photographer even appeared one day to take pictures because nobody could believe that so many people could fit on a shop floor. It was hell on wheels!*

One of the musicians who found work in the shop was John McLaughlin. Few would dispute John McLaughlin's reputation as being one of the greatest pioneers of jazz-fusion guitar of the 20th century.

Born in Doncaster, North Yorkshire in 1942, McLaughlin

first became interested in the guitar at the age of eleven, courtesy of his concert violinist mother. He promptly immersed himself in the playing of the Belgian jazz guitar pioneer Django Reinhardt.

As many like him did, McLaughlin moved to London around 1960 to find work and, in combination with undertaking whatever session or gigging work that was available, he supplemented his income with a job as a salesman at Selmer - probably in early 1961.

John McLaughlin: *What I do remember is Sam being a uniquely peaceful man and he certainly had a very different vibe from all the other people in Selmer at that time. Of course, most of the others were salesmen like me and were working on commission, so it was a hustle. He worked in what can only be called a cubbyhole in the basement at Selmer, but I was always happy when I needed to go down there so I could chat with Sam. He had a kind of oriental serenity that made me feel good just talking with him.*

In 1963, as well as finding time to teach a young Jimmy Page, McLaughlin joined his first band proper - the Graham Bon Quartet - which comprised him, Jack Bruce and Ginger Baker.

In 1969, he recorded his solo debut record, Extrapolation, before moving to America to play with, among others, Miles Davis and Tony Williams, in his band called Lifetime.

It wasn't until the formation of his electric band – the Mahavishnu Orchestra in 1971 - that McLaughlin would start pushing the jazz-fusion envelope for real. The band had two or three stints across the '70s and '80s that involved multiple line-up changes, but regardless, it served to cement McLaughlin's position as one of the world's greatest guitarists. Jeff Beck once called him 'the greatest guitarist alive.'

Doug Ellis: *John is an absolute great of jazz music nowadays. He's played with Miles Davis and goodness knows who else! John was another very likeable chap. He was very quiet and reticent. Back in those days I mostly just envied his good looks: slim, dark and quietly spoken. He was a very, very good-looking young man, and I always wished I'd looked like that. I'd have got a lot more girlfriends if I did!*

John McLaughlin: *Sam would show me certain chords on the guitar and speak about music in general. He certainly knew everything about guitars and taught me much in that direction.*

He was also helpful in my approach to harmony and introduced me to the American vocal group The Four Freshmen. This exposed me to the harmony being developed by Stan Kenton and his orchestra and subsequently put me on the path towards Gil Evans and his association with Miles Davis. Because of my affection for The Four Freshmen, I subsequently became a great admirer of the vocal group Take 6 and their further development in harmonic movement, all of which was originally stimulated by knowing Sam Li.

Doug Ellis: *Sam was also a very fine and very tasteful guitarist. Being a jazzer myself, I always liked to see people playing fancy chords that made your eyes water. Sometimes if he was sitting waiting to talk to you, he'd pick up a guitar and start playing these beautiful chords - thoughtful, gentle, wonderful music he used to play.*

Fiona Beattie: *At no point did I ever hear Sam say anything that suggested that he rated himself as a guitarist. He couldn't read music but he could play absolutely anything. He*

23

always played his abilities down.

It's hard to imagine many greater accolades than having taught a player like John McLaughlin. With hindsight, how could anyone offer anything to the man who seemingly knew all there was to know? Yet, Sam Li was able to give the great man a few things to add to his jazz palate.

However, it's highly unlikely that this friendly, understated interaction in Selmer's basement between these two young men who loved jazz carried any great significance at that time. This kind of transfer of information between aspiring young players was apparently quite normal.

Players, particularly jazz men, played - and did so communally without inhibition. Guitar shops were one of the places where they could do so. And this is one of the reasons why the '60s yielded forth so many great guitar players.

Doug Ellis: *There was great camaraderie in those days. Nearly everyone was a gigging amateur guitar player of some kind - myself included. I first got lessons at the age of nineteen from a chap that worked there called Brian Gilboy. He played in the orchestra pits and did all sorts of gigs. It was him that got me started playing guitar. It wasn't long before I was playing five nights a week and working five and a half days.*

Roger James – The Roger James 4 (Sam Li's friend and former session musician, including the Beatles): *Between about '62 and '67, they all worked there: Paul Kossoff, John McLaughlin and Jerry Donahue. Whenever I went in there, they'd be playing a guitar when there were no customers. Whenever anybody came in to buy something, they'd say, 'OK, I'll get that out of the case for you.' Jerry Donahue was a Canadian or American and I* *think he was later in Pentangle and those electric folk bands from the '60s and '70s.*

Everybody looked up to John McLaughlin especially. At that time they all played guitar all the time - that's why so many became great. They were all so good and every hour they were up and awake they were playing the guitar. That's why Hendrix was so good, because they say that even when he's cooking his breakfast, when he's got his eggs frying, he's got his guitar still round his neck; constantly playing. Jeff Beck said he's only ever been without a guitar once for three days and he felt like a wreck. He's got to have a guitar in every room so he can just pick it up.

By 1961 Sam Li had a home, a paying job and continued playing jazz. Having left Guiana just a couple of years earlier with only a vague hope of a brighter future, his life was indeed taking serious shape.

He could not have known that the world of music, a world in which he now truly belonged courtesy of his position at Selmer, was about to undergo one of its most rapid expansions.

Fortunately, Sam Li was a few steps ahead of many in terms of knowledge and craftsmanship skills. Those hours spent making furniture in his beloved Guiana had not been wasted. Consequently, he would be well placed to benefit when the rock music industry broke forth. Meanwhile, out of the blue, romance intervened.

Fiona Beattie: *My father, John, was a copywriter in advertising and my mother, Babs, was a French translator at the London telephone exchange. My parents' marriage broke down and I think my mother left my father in early or mid-1961.*

Some time afterwards, Pauline, a friend at the telephone exchange, invited my mother to a party and that's where she met

Sam - Pauline was Eddie Leu's brother-in-law's wife. Having been introduced and become aware of each other's musical abilities, they must have hit it off immediately. My mother and Sam married in March 1962 and Sam moved in to the family home. This was an era where interracial marriages weren't just uncommon but were actually frowned upon. As such, my mother and Sam married in secret and only told people, family included, that they had done so after the event. I was just barely two at the time.

'Baby who ah cry ah house, and ah door, ah di same thing'
(Look after someone else's child as you would your own.)

Having moved into his new family's home soon after the private wedding, Sam Li focused on using his career to create a solid foundation for his wife and stepchildren. As such, the period between 1961 and 1968 was not only pivotal in the context of the world of popular culture but these were also the vitally significant formative years of Sam Li's career trajectory.

Rock and roll music in its pure form was gradually being intersected by all manner of tricked-up extensions: blues rock, psychedelic rock, progressive rock to name but a few.

In parallel, singer/songwriters appeared on the scene in serious numbers, brimming with creativity and inspiration. Meanwhile, under Selmer's roof, Sam Li was well on his way to becoming known as the go-to person for guitar setup in London.

Doug Ellis: *Sam was by far the best (and certainly the most meticulous) guitar repairer and builder I ever met in my many years in the music business. When someone took a job to Dick Clifton, Dick would sort of grunt and say something like, 'I'm sure I can bodge it together somehow.' Sam was the opposite.*

When he took it away, you knew it would come back better than before.

For the uninitiated, guitar setup is a curious art. There are many elements that interlink. Some of them are tangible from a mechanical/electrical perspective. Others are vague, personal and somewhat intuitive. Principally, though, a guitar must be tuned. However, while a guitar may sound in tune and might even play in tune, because of the complexities of string length and bridge settings, it might not actually be in tune.

These vagaries are so subtle but at the same time so important. Furthermore, one musician's realisation of intonation can be very different from another's. This is where both a setup guy's understanding of the mechanics of intonation and his cognizance of each musician's preferences come to the fore as one. A guitar - and by extension perhaps its player - is only as good as its setup.

In simple terms, without overcomplicating matters, intonation refers to the accuracy of pitch. Intonation can either be flat or sharp. Several factors influence intonation - and, therefore, pitch accuracy - on a fretted instrument like a guitar.

The first of those is the depth of the strings in the slots at the guitar's nut (the string support position at the headstock end of the neck). Occasionally these slots are not cut deep enough with the result being that, if the string height at the nut is higher than at the fret, some pitch variance occurs.

Bridge position and the location and nature of the frets themselves are other factors that affect intonation. By the 1960s, most guitars would have had fully screwdriver adjustable bridges. Some had floating bridges, with position secured by string tension, whereas others had fixed bridges that had to be filed and shaped by the setup specialist to alter the contact point of the strings.

The guitar frets, each representing a semitone on the guitar neck, also play an important role in terms of a how a guitar sounds. Fret buzz - when the guitar's action (string height from bridge to nut) is too low - has always been a source of great annoyance to guitarists because it not only causes poor sound but it also drastically curtails the sustain of a note. Any contact that interrupts a string's natural vibration will inevitably cause a note to prematurely decay. Frets, being metal, are particularly capable of affecting a vibrating guitar string.

With excessive play, metal strings will eventually cut grooves in the frets too. In less severe cases, a guitar repair expert might 'dress' (level and polish) the frets as a temporary measure. In more extreme cases, the specialist would completely replace the frets.

In addition to setting up a guitar from an intonation perspective to suit each individual musician's needs and playing style, a setup and repair specialist like Sam Li would have been responsible for almost every other aspect of guitar maintenance. This would include structural repairs to the neck, body and headstock and the associated cosmetic paintwork/lacquering, neck twist rectification and truss rod adjustment, electrical adjustments to the pickups and associated volume and tone controls and, of course, more day-to-day jobs such as string replacement and neck inlay maintenance work.

All of these repairs and adjustments would have been commonplace to Sam Li. And with all these skills at his disposal, instruments belonging to some fairly influential musicians would inevitably pass through his hands. One such instrument was a 1959 Gibson Les Paul Standard that belonged to a young, softly spoken guitarist who went by the name of Peter Green.

Born Peter Allen Greenbaum into a Jewish family in Bethnal Green in 1946, Green's elder brother Michael reputedly taught him his first rudimentary guitar chords when he was eleven years old. He caught the bug. By the age of fifteen, he had taught himself and was already on the brink of playing professionally.

Surprisingly, Peter Green began his professional musical career not as a guitarist but as a bass player in a band called Bobby Dennis and The Dominoes - a pop outfit that performed pop and rock 'n' roll covers by acts like The Shadows. In later life, Green has been known to say that Hank Marvin was his guitar hero while growing up.

Green's big career break came in 1966 when Eric Clapton took temporary leave from John Mayall's Bluesbreakers. Green was asked to fill in for a series of live shows, after which he was asked to join the band on a full-time basis when Clapton's absence became permanent and he went on to join Cream.

For anyone, Clapton's shoes would have been hard ones to fill. But with time, Peter Green would become nothing less than a blues guitar legend himself, having developed a unique playing style that favoured swinging shuffle-grooves and minor-key phrasing that hinted at the dark side of his beloved blues.

Perhaps his best known recordings were in the early incarnation of Fleetwood Mac, which was formed in 1967 after Green too departed his position in John Mayall's Bluesbreakers.

Although Fleetwood Mac would achieve greater commercial success after Green's departure in 1970 and the creation of essentially a new band (indeed some casual observers might not even be aware that Peter Green was ever even in Fleetwood Mac), those early days of the band are still viewed with great fondness by the purists. It was, however, during these three years that Peter Green became synonymous with the Gibson Les Paul Standard.

To understand Green's guitar, one must also understand its origins within the context of what was happening in the electric guitar arms race of the time.

The Gibson Guitar Company, based in Kalamazoo, Michigan, first produced the iconic Les Paul shape in 1952. Founded in 1902 by luthier Orville Gibson, the company was initially focused on the manufacture of mandolin type instruments.

By the 1930s, the company was making flattop acoustic guitars to fulfil the demand triggered by the big band era, with the first hollow-bodied electric guitars appearing soon afterwards. And then everything changed. In 1948, the company hired businessman Ted McCarty who, after becoming president of the company in 1950, led the organisation into vast expansion.

The primary area of expansion was the electric guitar line, with input from famed country, jazz and blues guitarist of the time, Les Paul. To rival Fender's development of their Broadcaster and Esquire models, McCarty and his team developed the first Gibson Les Pauls, with the intention to create an expensive, high quality guitar that was not only in keeping with the company's reputation, but was also distinct from Fender models of that time.

Development of Gibson's flagship electric guitar continued throughout 1951 with various prototypes appearing that closely resembled the Les Pauls of today. The first model proper, the Goldtop, with two single-coil pickups, was debuted onstage by Les Paul himself at the Paramount Theatre in New York in June 1952. The blueprint for all future models was then established and the general specification included a solid mahogany body with a carved maple top and a single cutaway (an indentation adjacent to the guitar neck).

A year later, a second model, the Les Paul Custom, was released onto the market. This was a striking black variant with eye-catching gold hardware. Various enhancements were added in 1953 and 1954, the most significant and enduring being the Tune-o-matic bridge.

Instead of a fixed, wraparound bridge which was limited in terms of making adjustments for string length and thickness, this new 'floating' bridge allowed for far more adjustment courtesy of an oblong saddle with six saddle inserts.

Thereafter, lengths of string available to produce actual sound could, therefore, be adjusted within certain parameters and it was the string tension that held the bridge in place. With the exception of some entry-level models, the Tune-o-matic bridge system has been a standard fixture on the majority of Gibson electric guitars since the 1950s.

1958 heralded the first significant design change when the Les Paul Standard was introduced. While retaining many of the Goldtop's basic features and sitting squarely in between it and the Custom in terms of price-point, the Standard was available only in a cherry sunburst colour in the 1950s. A more rare edition with a tobacco sunburst finish followed later.

It should be said that in the initial years of Les Paul production through the early-mid 1950s, sales figures weren't exactly prolific. People weren't collecting guitars and admiring the contours with a view to them having any kind of future value.

Doug Ellis: *In those days, the idea of collecting - or indeed owning - more than one guitar just didn't occur to anyone. Most people started with something inexpensive, in my case a fifty-pound Hofner. Then, when you wanted something else or by some miracle could afford a Gibson or a Fender on hire purchase, you would either part-exchange your first guitar or sell it. People would only ever have one guitar. With retrospect, I wish I'd bought a few back then and stuck them in a cupboard. But of course I couldn't afford it!*

So, the primary consideration in the '60s was what a

guitar sounded like when it was plugged in. Playability trumped aesthetics every time. And given that the guitars were initially targeted primarily towards jazz players and were considered heavy and unwieldy by pretty much everyone else, sales were initially quite slow. Consequently, because of the Les Paul's sedate uptake, only approximately 1700 Les Paul Standards were made between 1958 and 1960.

Even in 1959, the year that is now considered to be the guitar's best vintage, Gibson only sold 643 Standards along with another 246 of the black Customs. Despite these relatively small sales statistics, Gibson still retained the largest market share of any manufacturer of electric guitars.

Gibson's main competitor in the 1950s, and this is still the case today, was Fender. Originally called Fender's Radio Service, the company we now know as the Fender Musical Instruments Corporation arrived a little later on the scene than their principal rival.

Having spent some years repairing radios, home audios and PA systems, the company founder, Leo Fender, entered into a partnership in 1941 with guitar designer and engineer Doc Kauffman. Together, they built amplification and musical instruments under the K & F Manufacturing Corp moniker.

Design and testing followed. Only in 1945 did production start in earnest, with a range of Hawaiian lap steel guitars that incorporated patented pickup and amplifiers being sold as sets.

After Fender and Kauffman parted ways the following year, reputedly due to differing visions as to the company's best direction, the organisation was then renamed Fender Electric Instrument Company.

During the late 1940s, Leo Fender experimented with more conventional guitar designs. The first of these, the Broadcaster, which initially boasted a warp-prone one-piece neck, evolved into the Esquire - with a bolt-on neck. This not only solved the warping issue but also, crucially, allowed the two main guitar components to be manufactured separately and by a relatively unskilled workforce.

In 1951, development of what we now know as the Telecaster - the first solid-bodied electric guitar in history - was complete, beating Gibson to the market by several months in the process.

From there, Fender just kept pushing the envelope. In 1954, the company released the Stratocaster guitar - to this day the most popular and copied solid-bodied electric guitar shape in history.

Unlike its Telecaster sibling, which was often criticised as being of plain, plank-like construction, the Strat was a completely different entity, with its softly contoured lines, body-hugging form and double-cutaway horn shape allowing complete access to the upper reaches of the fret board. The guitar had perhaps a more sensual appearance than its main competitor, the tough, uncompromising Les Paul.

While both guitars had their respective supporters, sonically the two most iconic electric guitars in history were poles apart. Where the Les Paul's twin humbuckers offered powerful, dirtier tones, the Stratocaster's three single-coil pickup system, while brighter in general terms, offered players a variety of tone according to which combination of the three were engaged - including one caused by a phenomenon known as phase-cancellation, where the middle and bridge pickups operated together with the pickup selector switch in certain positions.

Unlike the Les Paul, Stratocasters came with a bridge-mounted tremolo arm that could be moved to modulate the pitch. From 1954 onwards, therefore, the Stratocaster and the Les Paul would go head to head in the quest to be the guitar players' instrument of choice.

In 1965, Leo Fender sold his interest in the company to the broadcasting firm CBS for a figure reported to be in the region of thirteen million dollars. As a barometer of the scale of this deal at the time, that figure was significantly more than the company had paid for the New York Yankees baseball team a year previously.

Initially, the sale was considered to be a positive move for Fender's fortunes. CBS undoubtedly had powerful buying power and the ability to scale the business far beyond where it had been previously. However, with retrospect, purists now consider the buyout to have had a negative impact on the actual build quality of the instruments – to the extent that nowadays, as much as the '58, '59 and '60 models are the most desirable Les Pauls, it's the pre-CBS Stratocasters – particularly the 1962 models – that excite collectors and players most.

CHAPTER FOUR

While Buddy Holly undoubtedly cemented the Strat's desirable status throughout the 1950s until his untimely passing in 1959, it wouldn't be until 1964 that the Les Paul guitar shape's fortune really changed.

While others had championed the Les Paul's cause prior to that, including Les Paul himself, the moment Keith Richards first played a '59 sunburst Les Paul Standard - a guitar that had apparently sat unwanted on Selmer's sales floor for the best part of two years - was when other musicians began to recognise the guitar's potential.

And it happened almost overnight. In Richards' hands, his guitar – now known as the 'Keith-Burst'- was first seen at a now legendary Rolling Stones performance at the Palace Ballroom in Douglas, Isle of Man on August 13th 1964.

Thereafter, the guitar was seen regularly on stage, most notably on their UK tour in the autumn of 1964 and then later on the Ed Sullivan show on October 25th that same year. This high profile US television debut must surely have sealed the deal for the Les Paul Standard's iconic status.

Thereafter, the '58, '59 and '60 model years became the most sought after vintages. Nowadays they are, without doubt, the holy grails of Les Pauls - (a) because they're very, very good and (b) because there were relatively few made.

Greeny, as Peter Green's Les Paul Standard would affectionately be called, was one of these models manufactured in 1959. With serial number 9-2308, it was reputedly purchased by Green from Selmer for a sum reported to have been as little as £150 towards the end of his Bluesbreaker days - possibly sometime in late 1966 or early 1967.

Green initially played the guitar live and recorded with the band, but then began to express dissatisfaction with the performance of the neck pickup. Another story from the time hinted that Green, having seen Eric Clapton play his own '59 Les Paul almost exclusively on the bridge pickup, wanted the neck pickup removed altogether.

Either way, as any professional musician of the time would have done, Green took the guitar to the best specialists in town. He walked into Selmer Musical Instruments Ltd and requested that the neck pickup problem be investigated.

Much like any other job, the guitar would have been tagged, a receipt filled and returned to the customer. The instrument would have been taken downstairs to the experts in the setup department whereupon the job would have been assigned to whoever was available. Peter Green's guitar went in that day as just a Les Paul with a faulty pickup. It was simply another job. But when it came out, it was a phenomenon.

The key to 9-2308 was its tone. Simply put, after it left Sam Li's custody in 1967, it sounded like no other Les Paul. Indeed, it sounded like few other guitars period. Often described as out-of-phase, Greeny possessed a richness of tone that gave early Fleetwood Mac songs like 'Black Magic Woman,' 'Oh Well' and 'Albatross' an off-kilter atmosphere all of their own. Rather than sounding like a Les Paul, Greeny possessed a somewhat hollow tone that many said was more akin to that of a Fender Stratocaster which was rather ironic given the two companies' on-going rivalry.

The reason for this altered tone?

Well, it's a little complicated...

The 1959 Gibson Les Pauls came fitted with two humbucker pickups - one at the neck (bass) and one at the bridge (treble) - as a substitute for the P90 single-coil pickups that had been fitted to previous models. Although the earlier single-coil pickups were thought to offer a brighter sound than their humbucker equivalents, they were also liable to pick up the hum of other unwanted noise. This became a particular issue in a crowded room where musicians played in a group. The new humbucker, however, did what its name suggested: it bucked the hum created by electromagnetic interference.

At some point during the Selmer repair, the faulty front (neck) pickup on Green's guitar was removed for inspection. What was actually found when the pickup recess was opened up? We'll never really know. One theory suggests that the pickup was simply faulty and/or needed the wire coils rewound. Another claims that it was simply a case of the pickup recess in the guitar body being poorly shaped, causing the pickup itself to sit in a position that affected the output.

Whatever the issue, when the pickup was inspected and subsequently replaced, it was wired (or mis-wired whichever way you look at it) in such a way that when the guitar was played with the two humbucker pickups set in the middle position, Greeny's sound was completely transformed. In addition, it was claimed that the magnet in the same pickup had seemingly been inadvertently re-installed in reverse. Two presumably innocent mistakes led to one remarkable outcome.

Predictably, given the enthusiasm that guitar aficionados have for famous instruments and their various nuances, there has been much debate over the years as to precisely how and why Peter Green's Les Paul ended up being altered in such a way that, while seemingly subtle in nature, had such a fundamental effect on its playability.

And there was another question too: who had done this work?

Rumours abounded for years. Green himself has mostly downplayed the subject (and the guitar generally) and has often said that he doesn't really remember the details. At one point he was reputed to have described the guitar as a 'funny old fuddy-duddy with a neck like a tree trunk.'

Peter Green was respectfully contacted for this book but was unable to offer further information beyond the fact that the guitar was taken to Selmer for repair at some point because of an issue with the bass pickup.

One name that kept cropping up, however, was that of Sam Li – spelled in a variety of imaginative ways on a whole number of guitar forums: 'Sam Lee,' 'Stan Lee,' 'San Lee Guy' being just a few. Though the names varied in their spelling, the story was always the same: this was the guy who'd worked on Peter Green's guitar.

'If oil ah float watah deh ah battam'
(A little evidence can tell a whole story.)

On paper, everything about the association fitted perfectly. Sam was indeed working in Selmer's basement in 1967 when the guitar was handed in for repair and was, as mentioned, the favoured setup man.

Beyond that, we now know that there were certain subtle but crucial hallmarks associated with the repair work that just screamed Sam Li as loudly and clearly as Peter Green's '59 Les Paul Standard did in that middle pickup position.

Phil Harris: *It wasn't a modification; it was basically a* *cock-up! If you look at early shots of Green with John Mayall's Bluesbreakers, you'll see the bass pickup and the pole pieces - everything was as it would be on a regular Les Paul. Later, the bass pickup had stopped working because, back in those days, in a lot of these pickups the windings were wound way too tight. Eventually they broke.*

So when the bass pickup stopped working, Peter gave it to Selmer and it ended up with Sam. Sam then rewound it but he rewound it with the wrong gauge wire. He also put a leader cable on it that's nothing to do with a Gibson - it's like a plastic, shielded piece of cable. It's totally wrong for a humbucker pickup.

So he fitted the wrong leader cable and he used coil winders more suited to Fender pickups than Gibson humbuckers. One good thing he did was under-wind it. That's good for tone. I don't think that any of this was a conscious effort either. I just think that's what he thought was best at the time. And then the final thing he did was put the magnet under the coils in the wrong way round! That reverses the polarity, which basically creates an out-of-phase type sound when you put both pickups together. And then he put the pickup in the wrong way round so when you see the pickup, instead of the pole pieces facing the neck, they're facing to the bottom. Both pickups are facing the same way. It was a combination of mistakes.

Whether he actually meant any of the above or not, we'll never know. But really it seems unlikely. What is certain though is that, via an odd sequence of events, Sam Li's handiwork in Selmer's basement sometime in 1967 served to modify a guitar that would become nothing short of iconic as time passed.

You could argue that something of Sam Li's energy was unwittingly passed down the generations from that day forward. His hands touched the wires; the wires still transmit sound via the pickups today.

With a bit of investigation and various pieces of conversation with those who knew of him and his habits, a clearer picture of Sam Li's specific skills began to emerge. According to his stepdaughter, Fiona, the man loved electronics.

Gadgets generally fascinated him - *'He loved technology and always had the latest audio and television equipment,'* she recalls. A little ironically perhaps, according to some of his peers and experts on the London guitar scene, electronics were definitely not Sam Li's strong suit when it came to guitar repairs.

Phil Harris: *His electronics were apparently pretty bad. I heard he really struggled with it. Really, he was a woodwork man not a wiring man, but in the day then, back in late '67, he would have just turned his hand to whatever was involved in the job.*

Steve Clarke (guitar technician, journalist): *People that work with guitars have different strengths. I can do re-sprays, and I will do them if I have to. But I know guys who can do them better than I can. But with Sam it sounds like, while he had a degree of knowledge of electrics and wiring and wouldn't shy away from doing it, his real strength was on the wood side of things. In that area, I know he was very, very good.*

I also know that he almost certainly did the work on Peter Green's guitar because I later saw the wiring on a guitar Sam built from scratch that was played by Slade's Dave Hill. It's a fascinating instrument, and the overall build quality was wonderful, but the soldering really wasn't very good! I've looked closely at Peter Green's guitar. About four years ago, in an old mill in Stockport, Greater Manchester, the guy who was selling it, Richard Henry, gave me a call. I only had a very short time with it but remember the front pickup wiring having a grey outer insulation going to the control cavity. It reminded me immediately of Dave Hill's guitar in that the wiring to the famous neck pickup is almost identical to the wiring on Dave Hill's guitar. In fact, the piece of grey wire that comes from underneath the humbucker shouldn't even be there. It's the kind of wire you might find in a DIY store to fix your grandmother's table lamp. The same wiring is in both guitars! But it worked.

At the time, it's quite possible that once Peter Green's guitar left Sam Li's care in Selmer's basement in 1967, neither party gave it much further thought. As the years passed, however, the guitar's sound and reputation became more fully formed. Courtesy of Green's early Fleetwood Mac output the '59 Les Paul Standard steadily took on an aura of legend. And its passage through the eras had only just begun...

As the story goes, shortly before Green left Fleetwood Mac in 1970, he loaned the guitar to Irish guitarist Gary Moore who, at the time, was a teenager and relatively unknown. Moore was seemingly a fan of Green's playing and had befriended him on the road, all of which ultimately led to a transaction being agreed whereby Moore would purchase the Les Paul for the same price paid by Green a few years earlier. The number was again said to be in the region of £150.

Mark Moffatt (former manager of Top Gear, Denmark Street): *I was in the shop the day Gary bought Peter's guitar. He brought it in to show it off to us pretty much immediately after he'd picked it up. We all discussed the out-of-phase pickup. Gary didn't know the specifics of the electrics but he confirmed that it was Sam Li who had worked on the guitar.*

Having bought the guitar from Green, it wasn't as if Gary

Moore locked the '59 Les Paul Standard in a glass display case and gazed lovingly at it every hour on the hour.

On the contrary, Moore worked the instrument extremely hard - to the extent that sweat from his pick hand eventually wore the lacquer off the guitar's body. Greeny was Moore's day-to-day gigging guitar for much of his career - a career that included a debut solo album in 1973, a brief stint in Thin Lizzy during 1974 with a return in 1978/9, and then further hard rock-orientated solo records, followed finally by a series of blues albums. The latter amounted to something of a late career return to his roots. One of those albums was entitled Blues for Greeny.

There's a story that circulated about a meeting between Green and Moore sometime in the early '80s. Peter had apparently been playing a little guitar again and had, by chance, ended up in the same studio where Moore was recording. As the two talked, Green noticed Greeny on a stand in the room. As the two left the room, Green apparently passed his hand gently across Greeny's strings as he walked out - as if, as Moore later intimated, to restore something of himself back into the guitar.

Phil Harris: *I heard through the grapevine that Peter Green never really liked that guitar after Gary Moore had it because Gary thrashed the life out of it on all accounts. Peter reputedly liked shiny-looking, new guitars and Greeny wasn't ever like that after Gary had it.*

As time passed, Greeny's colour changed, not just because of Moore's unrelenting usage. There was another specific reason for this gradual transformation: the aniline dye originally used to create the cherry red aspect was sensitive to UV light.

Consequently, Greeny - and indeed many of that era's Standards - have faded to reveal more of a soft lemon colour, with any darker traces of the original cherry only visible beneath the pick-guard if fitted. In Greeny's case, no pick-guard was ever used. Peter Green apparently had it removed when he first bought the guitar from Selmer.

Money problems ultimately forced Moore to sell the guitar in 2006 for a figure reputed to be in the region of a million pounds. Sadly, Gary Moore passed away in 2011 at the age of just 58. His guitar, however, survived him.

Jol Dantzig (Hamer Guitars co-founder): *My recollection of the Peter Green guitar is limited but vivid, as it was only for a few hours in the 1970s. I do remember how stoked Gary was to have acquired it - he took it out of the case right on the street in front of his hotel when I picked him up! We went to the Hamer shop and I gave him the tour of the place. Then we went into the front office and I hooked him up into one of my vintage Marshalls to check out Greeny. He was playing all these Fleetwood Mac riffs, doing his very best PG impression, which was quite good. We passed the guitar back and forth, with me trying in vain to keep up. It was just two Fleetwood Mac fans geeking out like little kids, not believing their luck to be alone with such a famous guitar.*

The subject of the out-of-phase middle position came up because it was so obvious. I suggested we take a look inside. Electrically, the controls looked fairly intact - there may have been a new lead on either the switch or one pickup. I can't say for sure but the wiring seemed to be correct in that it was soldered up correctly. I knew that the pickups were out of phase because I'd built hundreds of guitars with that configuration, not to mention having handled dozens of '57-'60 PAF LP Standards, ES-335s as a vintage dealer. It was unmistakeable on recordings and in the flesh. I suggested that we use a compass to check the magnetic orientation of the pickups and, sure enough, one magnet had been flipped 180°. This happened occasionally at the Gibson factory but it could have also easily been done inadvertently by a repairman. I can't remember for sure which one it was but my guess would be the neck pickup because it looked like it may have been worked on at some point.

Of course you can reverse the wires in the pickup internally if you disassemble the pickup but, if this was so and the magnet was flipped as well, you'd be back to in phase. Turning the entire pickup around in the guitar doesn't change the phase as some people have surmised incorrectly. Your story about the repairman would make sense to me. I'd be interested to know if the magnet has been checked by anyone else.

Still, even without the middle position sound, the guitar had a very particular sound among Les Pauls. They are all a little different. I'd been buying and selling PAF equipped guitars for 15 years at that point and I knew what they sounded like. Although the 1950s guitars had a certain timbre to them that sets them apart from the later models, they were indeed all a little different from each other, which is something that you know when you've played more than a few for extended periods. There was no doubt that Greeny was a stellar instrument and its provenance only magnified that fact. If you've had the pleasure of sitting with it for a few hours, you'll know what I'm getting at. I've owned 'Bursts that have been very, very good and some that have been exceptional. This one was the latter. Gary wasn't interested in selling it. I asked. Can't hurt to ask.

The interesting thing is that, as unmistakeable as those guitars are, when Gary wasn't attempting to mimic Green, the guitar sounded like Gary Moore - albeit Gary Moore playing a great sounding Les Paul. Every player has his or her own signature - good or bad. A great guitar can't save a hack but *it can inspire a master. Ironically, I met Green quite a few years later in New York. He was in love with a guitar that I had built for the Miller Beer Company around the same time Gary and I played the Greeny guitar.*

After eventually being sold by Gary Moore in 2006 to Phil Winfield at Maverick Music, the '59 Les Paul bearing Sam Li's handiwork found its way into the hands of one or more private collectors.

Phil Harris: *I had Greeny in my possession for nearly two years. I wasn't the official owner, more of a custodian. I've owned over seventy Les Pauls from the '58, '59 and '60 era. I think I've had more than anyone of that particular model. Contrary to popular conception, Greeny doesn't in my opinion have an unusually thick neck. It's not a slim neck but, to me, it always felt lovely. Although it's been snapped, the resonant tone remains great and the pickups are great although the outputs are really quite low and more tonal. Another interesting thing about Greeny is its headstock pitch. In relation to other '59s, Greeny's pitch is two degrees further forward.*

Even though things have been changed: the pots, tuners, the bridge and the jack socket plate...it's still definitely got something about it. Gary actually broke the original bridge and first replaced it with a chrome sixties bridge. Then, in the '90s, he put a reproduction Gibson ABR-1 bridge on there. Having played it when Gary first got it and then many years later, it definitely felt older but fundamentally the same.

As Greeny found new temporary owners, its reputation and mystique grew further until, seemingly unable to resist the urgings of one of his own guitarist heroes, it entered the world of

Metallica's Kirk Hammett in 2014.

Born in the San Francisco area in 1962, Hammett's mother is of Filipino descent and his father, also a merchant seaman like Sam Li, was of English, German and Irish ancestry. Like many younger siblings, Hammett first became interested in music via his elder brother Rick's record collection, which included albums by the likes of Led Zeppelin and Jimi Hendrix.

By the age of fifteen, listening to music just wasn't enough. The magnetic draw of playing an instrument was too strong and Hammett bought his first guitar from a Montgomery Ward catalogue. Shortly afterwards he upgraded to a 1979 Fender Stratocaster replica, followed by a further step up to a 1974 Gibson Flying V, apparently funded by endless hours working in his local Burger King restaurant.

As the earliest roots of the thrash metal movement gripped his native Bay Area in 1979/80, Hammett formed the thrash metal band Exodus - named by him after the Leon Uris novel of the same name - at the age of just sixteen.

In 1983, Hammett's fortunes changed. As Metallica travelled to New York to record their Metal Up Your Ass demo, the incumbent guitar player, Dave Mustaine, was fired from the band, reputedly due to excessive drug and alcohol abuse. Kirk Hammett was soon drafted in as Mustaine's replacement.

Metallica's legacy as the biggest heavy metal band in the history of music is hard to dispute. Ever since 1983, Kirk Hammett has been there while the band sold hundreds of millions of albums and played to fans in almost every country you can think of.

Along the way, Hammett has not only accumulated guitars, but he also became a keen student of the history of the instrument. While he is now an ESP-sponsored artist, with a whole raft of that brand's guitars at his disposal, Hammett also has other guitars to his name: a Jackson Flying V, a '68 Gibson Les Paul Custom, a Les Paul Standard, an Ibanez RG, a couple of guitars designed by German guitar maker Ulrich Tueffel and a Jackson Randy Rhoads.

Hammett, therefore, is undoubtedly a guitar aficionado – there's no other way of putting it. At last count he had sixteen instruments in regular use. His private collection contains significantly more.

Talking to Metallica members isn't always easy though. Quite understandably, their management company, Q Prime, is economical and highly judicious when it comes to arranging press opportunities. Metallica is, after all, one of rock's biggest bands. As such, the band members' time is short and valuable. They don't endorse just any project with their input.

Kirk was contacted over a period of a few months, with occasional polite nudges on social media and a couple of private messages to an email address that may not even have been his. Sam Li's story, with its origins in Guiana, was spelled out briefly - with particular focus on Sam's craftsmanship, the mystique that surrounded him and his work and, of course, his role in the backstory of one of rock music's most revered instruments.

No response came back initially. Zero.

Kirk was contacted again, this time using another route provided by the legendary and extremely gracious rock radio show host, Eddie Trunk - 'You're holding this guitar in your hands every other night,' as a more emotional appeal was offered, 'I think you'd appreciate this unique story!' was reiterated.

'Cool! Set it up through Q Prime,' came the response a few days later. 'I'll talk to you soon.'

Kirk Hammett (Metallica): *Jimmy Page was talking to a friend of mine once about Greeny and Jimmy turned round and* said: 'I know that guitar. Kirk should buy that guitar...'

Sometime later, I had just arrived in London and I called a guitar dealer who I'd known for a number of years. 'Hey, what are you doing tonight?' I said. 'Let's go out and grab some food.' 'Yeah, let's do that. But I have a few things I want you to look at,' he told me. 'Well what have you got?' I asked. 'Well, I have Peter Green's Les Paul...'

My first thought was that I had no intention of paying the two million dollar price tag that apparently accompanied the guitar. 'Oh, no, that's all hogwash,' my friend said. 'Let me just bring it to you and you can check it out.' He brought it over, along with a vintage Marshall combo and a Vox combo.

I plugged Greeny in and, after maybe six seconds, I realised that it was such a unique guitar in terms of sound. And what made it instantly appealing was that the neck pickup on its own was nice and creamy and fat, as we all know. The bridge pickup is really powerful but never muddy. But the real magic of the guitar was in the middle position because it's there that the two pick-ups become out of phase. It's totally different from any other Les Paul – it sounded like a Strat through a hundred watt Marshall!

It seemed that, even on first inspection, Kirk Hammett - a guitarist who'd seen and played literally thousands of guitars across his career, including other Les Paul Standards - was sensing Greeny's subtle possibilities. All of a sudden, having had no intention of ever actually buying the guitar that Sam Li had repaired many years prior, Kirk Hammett was finding Greeny's charms impossibly persuasive.

Kirk Hammett: *My mind started racing. I was thinking: 'This is really unfortunate that this is such a priceless guitar.' So I asked the dealer how much it actually was and he told me. I* *decided to buy it. And part of my commitment to the deal was that I could never really tell anyone how much I paid. Let's just say that it was quite manageable and it was not two million dollars. I think people thought I had two million dollars to just burn on a guitar! To me, the fact that it was Peter Green's guitar was obviously great. But the fact that it was also Gary Moore's guitar actually means much more to me. I was always a huge Gary Moore fan and he has been an influence on my playing throughout my musical life. He used that guitar on Black Rose, which is one of my favourite Thin Lizzy albums. And so, when I put that album on, I hear Greeny all throughout those songs. I hear her voice.*

One other time I was in a comic book store in New York, minding my own business looking at comic books. Next thing I know, I find myself looking up because I hear Greeny. There was a Fleetwood Mac song on the radio. I think I'm trained to hear it.

While the electrical aspects of Sam Li's work are still intact, thereby facilitating Greeny's sound, inevitably, given the guitar's age, there have been other subtle changes made over the years that a keen eye like Hammett's was never going to miss.

Kirk Hammett: *Guitars get better the more you play them. I know this to be true because I've taken ESP guitars right from the factory and, to start with, they can often be stiff and high-endy. But slowly, as you play them, the guitars start to come into their own. All the elements start to gel and come together and coalesce. Only then do guitars really start sounding great.*

All my best-sounding guitars are the ones I play most. My Mummy guitar - which fans know well - sounds great because I play the hell out of it. Guitars are tuned instruments, yes. But there are other things that contribute: being played, being heard and being approached with energy. And then I believe that guitars respond to that energy.

Greeny is certainly a player's guitar in that it's pretty beat up. I know for a fact that it has been broken twice in its life - on one occasion when it was in the trunk of Gary Moore's car when it got rear-ended. I'm told there was a crack right across the headstock between the A and D tuners. That was obviously fixed. There was other neck damage too, I believe.

There are other things that have obviously been changed and replaced too. The pickup switch cap has been changed numerous times – as have the guitar strap knobs. The tuners are now Schallers, I believe. Other than that, everything is pretty much as it has been since Peter Green's time.

It plays amazingly, stays in tune and has this nice thick neck, which means I don't need to worry about it much in terms of drastic temperature changes. If it had a thinner neck I'd have been a little more worried.

As far as when I use it, Greeny in the middle position is great: when you want to track two or three guitars and want to have a different voice, you can do that with the volume turned down on both pickups. There I get that Strat-type sound that lets me play rhythmic, bluesy and funky sounds. But turned up it's like a Strat full-on – I love that too.

Hammett's acquisition of Greeny was undoubtedly big news in the music world. On every level, he fitted the bill perfectly as far as being the right kind of custodian for such an iconic piece. Indeed, given his affinity with Moore, it was almost as if Greeny found Hammett as opposed to the other way around.

This suggestion raises a question which is often debated among those who both appreciate real craftsmanship and who can also get on-board with the idea that a guitar - on paper an inanimate object - can not only have some kind of subtle 'personality' of its own, but can also carry with it something of the energy of those who've both played it and worked with it in the past. Peter Green, Gary Moore and, of course, Sam Li fall into that category. Maybe Greeny is the conduit for the spirit of a few others too?

Kirk Hammett: *I've become aware of some of the guitarists who've played that Greeny guitar at various times over the years. In addition to its custodians, Jeff Beck, Rory Gallagher, George Harrison, Jimi Hendrix and Phil Lynott have all played it. As such, I'm a firm believer in quantum mechanics and the quantum world whereby, when anything comes into contact with something else, there's always an exchange of molecules, however small.*

Now, when you consider that all these people have touched and played this guitar, some of them for decades, then there has been a lot of mojo put into that guitar: sweat, determination, sentiment, vision and inspiration. Think about that. It has had the opportunity to sing for hundreds of thousands of people only recently. I took it on the stadium tour last summer and I'll take it again.

That guitar has had an active fan base that existed way before I ever came into contact with it. I get people coming to me all the time, saying: 'Where's Greeny?' If I can, I'll say, 'Play it, man. Play it as much as you want.' Usually they want a picture with it. And if they have a Les Paul of their own, they'll want a picture of the two guitars together. This has become routine with both my musician friends and people that I don't know at all. And I'm open to it all because, if any guitar on the planet is 'of the people,' it's that guitar. It belongs in a museum really - but it wouldn't be realising its full potential there. If it could speak, it would say: 'Let me out of this prison...'

Ever since it was created, its destiny was to be amongst people, being heard. And the reason is because, from the beginning, as a result of its history, it has stood out from all the others. Over the years it has been cared for by people with so much creative energy to give - so much sentiment, determination and sweat. And it has absorbed it all. These things added together make such a difference. That's what guitar players call mojo.

I feel like a custodian rather than an owner. It's just passing down the line. I know that feeling well and I'm comfortable with it as long as I get to hang out and play it every day. It's a special piece of wood. And it's right beside me now. It sleeps where I sleep.

Either way, Greeny has found the perfect home for now. Instead of being locked away in a case or hanging on an exhibition wall, Greeny is doing what Greeny does best: being played every other night.

In addition to regularly appearing on stage at Metallica shows, Hammett also used Greeny for tracking certain parts of the band's album, Hardwired To Self-Destruct, released in 2017. His mojo, one would assume, is being added to the guitar on a daily basis.

Steve Clarke: *It's quite well known that in psychic circles, someone can pick up a watch belonging to a person who has passed away and come up with a whole character reference. It's quite remarkable. Similarly, I've heard of people who receive organ transplants and inherit some of the traits of the donor. So, it wouldn't be a surprise to me that Kirk Hammett might be picking up some of the echo, the resonance, of the people who've handled the guitar before him.*

With his attachment to work carried out on one of music's most talked about guitars confirmed, it would be no exaggeration to suggest that Sam Li himself has become, by association, part of rock 'n' roll folklore.

While it seems likely that, given how busy Selmer's basement no doubt was in the late '60s, the work was done on a tight deadline, it seems reasonably certain too that his work on Greeny was carried out in entirely good faith and to the absolute best of his ability.

After all, nobody has ever questioned Sam Li's dedication to his craft or his attention to detail. Call it mojo, call it luck, call it whatever you like but, via a complex chain of well-intended errors, Sam Li cemented his place in guitar folklore just eight years after arriving on a flight from the Caribbean.

Phil Harris: *The beauty of some of these things, and this applies to all artists, is that it's not always about the perfection of technical ability. Sometimes it's that stroke of brilliance and what happens around that - that little unseen ingredient that makes something happen. Sam probably had an ear and, if he listened to it the wrong way round, to him it probably sounded right. So maybe he could hear something we all couldn't. But that's basically it. Peter Green and Sam are connected and, like in a lot of things in history, a mistake can end up being a stroke of brilliance. That's what that was. He had the hand of God.*

As a result of their mystique, the vintage era Les Pauls have inevitably been reissued in a variety of modern custom shop forms - both by Gibson themselves and by their related subsidiary company, Epiphone. Recently, Chinese-made replicas known as 'Chibsons' have appeared on the market at a fraction of the price of the real things.

Predictably, some of the reissues are extremely faithful to the original guitars, some less so. Some are even better...

Phil Harris: *There is a famous man, and he must remain nameless, who is the only man on Earth who can take vintage wood and make you an original Les Paul Standard. He's made me several. Let's just call him the Scarlet Pimpernel. Some of them I sell, others I keep. These aren't just replicas; these are actually better than some of the originals. They are that good. When I had Greeny, I gave it to him for six months and he made me an identical replica: the same weight, the same style of wood; he even broke the headstock off at the same point and re-glued it so that it had Greeny's defects as well. If you look at the two together, you'd never know the difference. In fact, on the Internet there are a couple of video clips of me playing the Greeny guitar. In at least one of those, I'm actually playing the replica. They are that similar. Every single nut, bolt and scratch is identical on each. On Greeny, after the neck was rebound following the break, one of the dots at the twelfth fret was bigger than the other. The replica is the same.*

CHAPTER FIVE

By 1968, having unwittingly modified and passed an iconic guitar down the generations from his cramped work space beneath Selmer's sales floor, Sam Li's career stood at another unexpected crossroads.

Between March 1968 and February 1969, a company decision meant that there was to be a progressive move to relocate many of the company's operations away from Charing Cross Road to a site outside Central London in Braintree, Essex.

As part of the plans, the distribution and sales office was to be moved from Charing Cross Road and the warehousing operation from a building in Clerkenwell. Similarly, a bespoke service department was then to be created in Braintree meaning that only the retail site would remain above where Sam Li had been working for the previous seven years.

For all involved, this undoubtedly would have come as a severe blow given that - on a surface level at least - the repair business had appeared to be very healthy. Who knows what was going on at a corporate level but the relocation was nevertheless rubber-stamped from above.

Whether some or all of the pre-existing setup staff were offered continuing positions at the new site in Braintree is not certain. Given the distances of travel involved, it would certainly have been a difficult decision to make for anyone like Sam Li who resided in central London.

As it turned out, Sam didn't relocate. Instead he left Selmer in the summer of 1968 and, thereafter, spent several months officially unemployed while doing occasional guitar repair jobs from home while assessing his future options, one would imagine. In January of 1969, something came up. Sam took a job working in some capacity at the BBC at the Television Centre in White City.

Soon fate or, perhaps more aptly near tragedy would change Sam Li's course again. After only a few of months working at the BBC, in what capacity nobody quite knows, a minor fire broke out in the family home.

Having dealt with the fire and burned his lower legs in the process, Sam was unable to go into work the following morning. For reasons unknown, Sam Li didn't even call in to explain what had happened. He just said nothing at the time and only called later. He was sacked soon afterwards.

Fiona Beattie: *The fire was in March 1969. Sam had come in to my bedroom in the morning to wake me and had, at the same time, put the electric heater on to warm my room. Houses didn't have central heating in those days. I got up and was in the living room while Sam was in the bathroom getting ready for work. I imagine that, through the bathroom window, Sam saw flames at my bedroom window. Suddenly he came flying out of the bathroom and ran straight into my room. I hadn't a clue what was going on but could hear noises coming from there. He came out after a good few minutes. I don't remember what he said but, when he sat down on the sofa, I could see his shins were burned. The curtains had seemingly caught fire and I imagine that he pulled them off the wall and they somehow burned his legs.*

He was more upset about losing his job than burning his legs. For me, being young, I felt terrible. Somehow I felt I was to blame. I always thought he should have just called his work and explained what had happened. 'Surely they'd understand?' I thought. But he was the adult and he knew best. He never called.

After a few weeks in recovery, Sam surely started considering his future options again. As proud as Sam would have been about working for such a respected company, whether a career with a large corporation like the BBC ever really appealed to him and his interests is open to question.

What's more likely is that Sam had a combination of autonomy and finances at the forefront of his mind. Given that he was fundamentally a quiet, introspective man, a solitary working environment whereby he could set his own pace was always going to be his preference.

Obviously too, he needed to protect his family by finding a way to pay the mortgage on the home which, by that time, was a purchased house in North West London. In his own way, Sam Li continually exhibited his love and care for his family.

Fiona Beattie: *Sam was a quiet man, and I was a very shy, quiet little girl, and so we didn't say a lot. Sam didn't express his emotions in words but would show his affections with deeds.*

One time, when I must have been around seven and was most unwell, the doctor said I should rest for several days. I was allowed to sleep during the day on the sofa and read my favourite comics and it was Sam who cooked home-made chicken soup for me.

Sam would sit with me and talk, trying to teach me about people, money and life. He would say that if you have to ask the price of something then you couldn't afford it. Or that one couldn't judge someone by his or her appearance. He would tell me about the scruffy rock stars who had turned up at his workshop in the most expensive cars.

Sam was always very generous but would try and teach me to wait for things. He asked me one day whether I would prefer a gold ring now or a bicycle later. I thought I'd chance my luck and said both now. He just smiled. I got the bike later.

To anyone else, Sam Li's direction, given his status in the music business, might have appeared obvious. Although Selmer was no longer active in its previous capacity, there were several other musical instrument shops in the area that might well have welcomed someone with Sam Li's expertise and reputation as the sixties music boom slowly edged towards the dawn of seventies rock.

Whether he ever actually used his many existing friendships and business acquaintances as a means of applying for a position elsewhere seems unlikely. Nobody recalls Sam Li making himself available for any other company during that time.

Instead, he struck out alone by renting a first floor premises above a Chinese restaurant called the Kowloon at 19 Gerrard Street, Soho - two or three doors in from its junction with nearby Wardour Street.

While Gerrard Street is now the very epicentre of modern Chinatown, in 1969 it wasn't even considered to be Chinatown at all. It was at that time, undisputedly, in the very heart of Soho.

Named after Baron Gerard of Brandon, Suffolk, who first commissioned the land in 1680, Gerrard Street became synonymous - as was the case with much of what was once known as Soho fields - with London's sex industry. This was the case from as far back as the middle of the 18th century following the departure of the aristocracy.

Although it is now the main route through modern Chinatown, Gerrard Street first saw an influx of just a few Chinese residents in the early 1920s but didn't become known as a neighbourhood popular with Chinese people until after World War II, when families were relocated there from other heavily bombed areas of London.

In the years following the war, Gerrard Street became known as one of Soho's main thoroughfares and, by the late '50s, it was home to little other than brothels, disreputable nightclubs and shops selling cheap books and magazines.

At 5 Gerrard Street, George Harrison Marks, a photographer synonymous with what we now refer to as glamour photography (used at the time as a subtle euphemism for 'nude'), opened a studio with his partner, Pamela Green, for a magazine called Kamera.

Around the same time, the West End Jazz club opened at 44 Gerrard Street. It was here that beatniks, layabouts and art school students took part in the first all-night raves.

After a couple of years, the Good Earth folk club moved in and shortly afterwards became 44 Skiffle Club, run by John Hasted. With his resident house band known as John Hasted's Skiffle and Folksong Group in situ, the club became the focus of what was considered to be one of the country's first youth movements geared exclusively towards music.

Concurrently, Gerrard Street - specifically number 39 - became synonymous with another significant club of the London music scene. Opening in 1959, Ronnie Scott's Jazz Club would become one of Soho's most important hotspots until its move to Frith Street in 1965.

Having become a dingy strip joint in the intervening years, 44 Gerrard Street then became a psychedelic club called Happening 44, run by a beatnik fellow by the name of John Braceland who, among other ventures, had previously run a nudist colony at Five Acre Woods near Watford.

With a fondness for elaborate light shows using Aldis

projectors and wet slides, Braceland's club would have indeed been happening by the time Sam appeared on Gerrard Street in 1969. Both Pink Floyd and Fairport Convention played some of their early gigs there in the late 1960s.

So, from this small upstairs room in late '60s Soho, in the midst of a frenetic music world, Sam would repair guitars for the players of the time. It was the dawning of both a new era in music and Sam Li's life.

* * *

'Nah put all two foot in river if yuh want see how he deep'
(Do not jump into a venture until you know that it is worthy.)

Whatever it was that pushed Sam Li in the direction of trading alone and being reliant on just the magic in his own two hands, it's unlikely that the decision was a mere speculative stab in the dark. While Sam reputedly liked a small bet on the horses now and again, he certainly wasn't one for taking reckless risks when it came to his and his family's livelihood.

What is much more likely is that during his time at Selmer, with a maelstrom of musical evolution swirling around him, Sam Li would have carefully assessed not only his current position but also what the picture could potentially be down the line.

Armed with that information, when fate intervened twice, courtesy of the Selmer restructuring and the short-lived BBC job, Sam would have known exactly what the earning potential was from a business perspective.

After all, in his eight years in Selmer's basement, he'd likely seen every kind of guitar repair job and, more significantly, the sheer volume of the footfall coming through the door. It would, therefore, have made sense to him that, given his contacts and reputation, there was no reason whatsoever why he too couldn't capitalise on a music explosion that was several years from being the figurative tail of the comet.

The customers were there and he had the expertise. Rent aside (and we don't know exactly what he paid), start-up costs would have been relatively low given that guitar men all had their own tools that travelled with them. Everything was in place. In 1969, it was now or never.

While his workshop was where the actual repairs happened, the transactions that initiated them were often instigated elsewhere - many of them within the squashed rectangle created by Wardour Street in the west, Shaftesbury Avenue to the north and Charing Cross Road a half mile to the east.

At the epicentre of it all, there was Denmark Street - often referred to as London's own version of Tin Pan Alley - which was once home to all manner of music publishers, management offices and rehearsal studios.

Having first been developed in the late 17th century and named after Prince George of Denmark, Denmark Street was initially little more than a slum – an impoverished area home to prostitutes, beggars and thieves. However, as part of a concerted gentrification effort aimed at London's West End in general, Denmark Street and the streets surrounding it were cleaned up significantly in the mid-19th century and, as part of this process, many of these previously seedy dwellings were converted ready for commercial use.

At the beginning of the 20th century, the first music publishers moved into the area and, by 1926, having started business a few years before World War I, Lawrence Wright launched the Melody Maker publication from number 11 Denmark Street - and was closely followed by another well-known music publisher of the time, Campbell Connelly.

By the 1950s, with the addition of the New Musical Express, who took up a position at number 5, Denmark Street was firmly established as the epicentre of all things music-related. Larry Parnes, an artist manager and impresario, had created a stable of young singers to manage from his Denmark Street office. Meanwhile, Lionel Bart - a pop music writer and composer of musicals such as Oliver! - became known as the King of Denmark Street.

During the years when Sam Li was employed at Selmer, Denmark Street was undergoing yet another personality change. When artists like the Rolling Stones realised that they could actually write their own songs, recording studio space became a more valuable commodity than freelance songwriters. Consequently, recording studios sprang up on Denmark Street - the first of which was Regent Studio at number 5 that opened in 1961 and was where the Rolling Stones recorded their debut LP in 1964.

In those days Denmark Street really was the street of dreams - broken or otherwise. The future hopes of many an artist really were either buoyed or dashed there, prompting Andrew Loog Oldham - the man who discovered and managed the Rolling Stones - to once describe it as 'Short, shabby Denmark Street, just off Charing Cross Road, an inhospitable place, full of brutish men.'

Loog wasn't wrong. This was Soho of the sixties - where the scope of the various goings-on within this small part of central London completely belied the area's size. There was mystery, character, danger; everything was available in Soho. By day there was an enormous proliferation of small shops and random businesses - far removed from the relatively organised commerciality of today's Chinatown.

Once the sun was gone from the sky, however, 1960s Soho

revealed a different, darker side to its ever-developing personality. Bars buzzed with musicians and wannabe actors; prostitutes were visible on the roadside. Exotic-looking Chinese people wandered the side streets selling all kinds of weird-looking food.

Nowadays we take this kind of cross-section for granted, of course, but 1960s Britain wasn't in any way cosmopolitan - to the extent that, once you left Soho, it seemed as if that world did not exist elsewhere. In those days it was a true microcosm - all of it in stark contrast to today, where shopping malls and apartment complexes prevail, and Chinatown's boundaries are clearly marked, in almost corporate style, with elaborate, wrought iron gateways.

By 1969, Soho was still the epicentre of everything creative. And while the various protagonists were often seen in person, deals that involved the lucky ones were being made and films and albums were being cut and produced in behind-the-scenes offices, studios and boardrooms far above street level.

When they weren't in pubs and clubs like the famous Giaconda Café at 9 Denmark Street - where musicians like David Bowie, Jimi Hendrix and Elton John would ultimately gravitate - musicians frequented the growing number of music shops in the vicinity: Macari Musical Instruments on Charing Cross Road, Top Gear on Denmark Street, Sound City at 22 Rupert Street or Sam Li's former employer, Selmer, at 114-116 Charing Cross Road. This demographic would form the core of Sam Li's customer base.

Phil Harris: *Sound City specialised in Fender and Selmers did Gibson in those days. They're totally different in almost every way and Sam had such an advantage because he could work on both of them. Back then, nobody wanted to play semi-acoustic guitars. Clapton played a Les Paul; Hendrix played a Strat.*

63

Rickenbacker and Gretsch were dirty words when I was a kid. To this day, Gibson and Fender are the only guitars I play.

Back then, nobody apart from Sam knew how to set up guitars in Central London. There were no guitar men. I remember walking into a guitar shop to buy my first Strat on HP. I tried five of them and they all played differently. Furthermore, I couldn't get the one that played the worst to play any better because there was nobody to do it. It was what it was and it played how it played. Nobody knew about fretwork in those days either. If notes choked, the only thing you could do was raise the action so high that you could hardly play it. Nobody knew what else to do.

Each of these music shops had their specialities and favoured brands to lead with. From a small, scruffy corner shop, Macari's sold Vox gear, in addition to their famous Tone Bender guitar pedal, which they sold in considerable quantities from 1965 onwards.

Sound City was owned by Arbiter Electronics, a manufacturing and distribution company and, after identifying an obvious opportunity to create their own line of sound-reinforced equipment, they did just that and set about designing and assembling them in the rear of their Rupert Street shop.

This range of gear, also named Sound City, included the Arbiter Fuzz Face distortion pedal which would later be used and endorsed by Jeff Beck and Jimi Hendrix.

As a result of his excellent reputation as a former setup guy at Selmer, the retail staff there would often direct the aspiring rock musicians of the day who were in search of specialist repair work - tasks that would have previously been performed in their own basement on a daily basis - to Sam Li's workshop on Gerrard Street, from where the distinctive smell of wood glue wafted its way down the stairs and onto the street below. Other music shops that knew of Sam and his abilities also referred business his way.

Pete Cornish (former service manager at Sound City on Shaftesbury Avenue): *I first met Sam when I was the service manager at Sound City on Shaftesbury Avenue. It was probably early 1970. He came in with an electric guitar that wasn't working properly and I just fixed it like a normal repair job. When he came in with another that wasn't working I questioned him, only to discover that he had made these guitars himself but his electronics were not as good as his obvious skills with wood were. I soon realised that it was going to be easier for me to do the wiring from scratch than for me to undo everything he'd done and start all over again.*

A great partnership developed. He was friendly and business-like but he never really discussed his life outside the business. And then, from that day on, I wired every guitar Sam built until he left Gerrard Street and Sound City sadly closed in 1975. I used to take these wired guitars round to his workshop up on the first floor on Gerrard Street. I seem to remember there was a Chinese gambling den in the building somewhere. I saw many fine examples of Sam's work on these visits. He made a solid Les Paul type guitar with a curved fret board that could be played with a violin bow. I believe it was made for Eric Faulkner of the Bay City Rollers. It was an incredible piece of craftsmanship.

So, rather than simply tapping his contacts for potential employment at their places of work, Sam Li was skilfully initiating symbiotic relationships that worked perfectly for all parties.

Given his relative shortcomings in this particular discipline of the trade, Sam would bring in electrical repairs that either needed a quick turnaround or were perhaps beyond his capabilities.

In return, Sound City would refer clients to Sam for wood and fretwork. Many other guitar shops in the West End would do the same. They all trusted Sam. They all grew to rely on Sam. Pretty soon, the workbench filled and the good times rolled.

Doug Ellis: *I left Selmer in late 1968 and got what I thought was a proper job working as a rep for the 3M Company. I absolutely loathed it and I was very frowned upon because I just couldn't take some of their sales training courses too seriously. I was without doubt the worst sales rep they ever had.*

Meanwhile, Brian Gilboy had also left Selmer in 1968 and had gone to work for the Dallas Arbiter group of companies, which were located in the West End. One was Sound City, another Drum City and there was also Modern Sound. In 1970, Brian Gilboy hired me as manager of Sound City - and I stayed there for a further three or four years.

We used Sam a great deal and there were a couple of reasons why we did. Firstly, he was so highly regarded. His attention to detail was so incredibly painstaking. Secondly, because he was such a great player; he also had a wonderful ear. In those days before strobe tuners, Sam Li's ear was the one to plug into.

Phil Harris: *I remember I worked as a Saturday boy in 1970 in Pan Music. It was above the Whiskey-A-Go-Go in Wardour Street, which was across the road from where Sam had his workshop in Gerrard Street. A guy called Pat Chapman ran Pan Music in those days and you could actually see Sam's workshop from the front window. If anything ever went wrong in there - if a neck was twisted or something was not right - I used to run them straight in to Sam's. He'd set them up, fix frets and would generally get them up and running again. I only worked Saturdays, so I'd run things over and then, when I came back to* *work the next Saturday, they'd already be back on the wall in our shop. Sam had worked on them during the week and returned them. He did the same for all the West End stores.*

I was only fifteen at the time and I'm sure he just thought I was a pest. I remember going in there one day and he had these two '50s Goldtops with P-90 pickups. 'I've got one of those,' I told him. 'Can I play one?' He just looked at me in that withering way that he did and said, 'No, you can't.' 'Whose are they anyway?' I asked him. It turned out that they belonged to Johnny Kongos, who had a couple of hits around that time.

John Kongos (musician): *Around that time I bought a 1955 Les Paul Gold Top from a South African guitarist friend who had acquired three of them in South Africa and brought them to London. His name was Mike Lentin. I was always in the guitar shops in London around that time. , I don't actually recall getting any work done on my guitar but he may have prior to my purchase. I still have that '55 Gold Top today though!*

CHAPTER SIX

Given his connections and, critically, his thorough knowledge of the two favoured guitar brands of the time, Fender and Gibson, not surprisingly and within a short period of time Sam Li surely had a steady stream of referrals. And with that, one would imagine, it's likely that he created an order book that stretched many months ahead.

All of a sudden, only a short time after leaving Selmer, amid circumstances that could well have become a little precarious for him and his family, Sam Li had reinvented himself. Not only was he earning excellent money and developing his reputation further, he was doing it in his own space and under his own terms.

Phil Harris: *He was the best known guitar man in the West End. There was Grimshaw's – which was basically a place you held a crucifix towards, bless 'em. Everything about them was not good. Dick Knight was cool but he was out in Byfleet so, unless you had a car and could afford to spend half a day to get there, it didn't work. All of us lived in Central London in those days, so Sam was literally the guy on the block. He was a one-stop deal. If you had a problem with your guitar, had any structural problems, needed a setup, needed the frets done or whatever it was, you went to see Sam. And when you gave him a guitar to set up, you absolutely knew it would come back playing really well.*

In those days, it was all like pit stops. And it wasn't a pit stop for me getting out to Byfleet. It was ridiculous to go all the way out there only to go back again and Dick was sort of known to be quite obstreperous anyway. He did some disastrous things with guitars too - like taking the binding off when he was doing re-frets. It would shrink and there'd be gaps at the top and bottom. And he was always busy because of his reputation of having done the Beatles' guitars. And the reason he did those was because it suited them to have their roadie, Mal Evans, take their guitars there because the Beatles couldn't really walk around Soho without being mobbed. These guys apparently lived out in nearby Weybridge anyway.

One question worth posing is whether there was any rivalry in the London guitar repair world at that time as a result of Sam Li branching out as an independent in his own premises.

Dick Knight was undoubtedly a well-established craftsman with top clientele - albeit in a location that was some distance out of town and required something of an effort to get to. How did he feel about Sam Li being the new kid on the West End's guitar block?

Dick Knight was born in 1907 and became a proficient amateur musician, playing the banjo and the clarinet recreationally while working as a machinist. During the War he worked for Saunders-Roe building bridges and pontoons, while at the same time tinkering with guitar making in the shed at the bottom of his garden.

In 1963, Knight started making guitars full time and, a year later, having repaired a guitar for Gordon Wells (who became romantically involved with and married Dick's daughter), the two took the Knight Guitar business forward with Dick making guitars and Gordon doing repairs.

The company was established and proven. But perhaps Sam's setting up business in Central London, in combination with his cosy relationship with West End retail outlets, took business away from Dick Knight? While competition in any industry is usually considered to be a healthy condition, was there some kind of simmering resentment as a result? It's hard to say.

What is true is that, when contacted, Dick's son-in-law Gordon Wells, who took over the business, had nothing good to say about Sam Li - specifically his electrical work.

Wells relates a story where, when asked about a guitar continually cutting out, Sam suggested the use of insulation tape. In isolation and without further context, this tale doesn't amount to much. But there's a sense Wells' take on that incident was a blanket inference that Sam's methods were all unconventional.

Mark Moffatt: *My contact with Sam was mainly dropping by his shop and chatting about the woodworking side of repairs. He knew where I worked - which is probably why he took the time to answer questions from a young bloke. His shop was on Gerrard Street, so it was an easy port of call when walking between Top Gear in Denmark Street and our other shop, Guitar Village, on Shaftesbury Ave.*

My job also entailed taking repairs out to Dick Knight near Weybridge and I have to say there was not much love lost between the two. Dick acknowledged Sam's luthier skills but, when the topic of electronic repairs came up, he unkindly referred to Sam as "the butcher of Gerrard Street."

Bernie Marsden (guitarist with Whitesnake, UFO): *In the early days Sam was the go-to man for any repairs! I always took my guitars to Top Gear in Denmark St. and I assume they were then passed to Sam to do any repairs because I used to see him in there and got to know him a little over the years.*

Without further explanation from Gordon Wells, we'll

probably never know the full story. But, given that almost everyone else in the scene at the time has been nothing but complimentary about Sam, there must be some possibility that the Dick Knight organisation saw Sam as some kind of threat from 1969 onwards.

Sid Bishop (guitar industry professional): *I was involved in the retail music instrument biz from the late '60s, right through until the early '90s, most of that being in Denmark Street and the surrounding vicinity - plus seven years at Chappell's of Bond Street. We didn't avail ourselves of Sam's talents very often. Of course I met him on one or two occasions, though I can't claim to have known him well, and generally we would only run a guitar repair down to Gerrard Street to see him if the job was an emergency or we needed it back in a real hurry.*

Ninety percent of our repairs were done by Dick Knight down in Byfleet. And then, in due course, Top Gear employed Roger Giffin - thus we then had our own in-house guitar technician who could adequately service our customers and our own stock. Once Roger had moved to the US in the '80s, I - or whichever shop I was working in at the time - went back to using Dick Knight again and, once he had sadly passed away, his son-in-law Gordon Wells carried on the tradition. I can't really say why we didn't use Sam more often. I suppose one just gets into a routine of using certain people to do certain jobs and, over time, you get to know them, trust them and have confidence in the quality of their work. So, why go anywhere else?

Phil Harris: *I didn't go to Sam via Selmer's or Sound City either. All the guys in the know just went straight to him. When Hendrix smashed a guitar up, or he set fire to a guitar and needed* *it put back together again or he broke a neck on one of his Strats at a show playing 'Purple Haze' or when he threw the guitar on the floor, it would have been Sam who would have had to repair that. Also, because he'd done work for Fender before, whenever a new neck arrived from Fender, it would have been Sam who had to put it on the body and set it all up. He would have worked for Hendrix.*

I went to see Sam in '71 to get my Les Paul put together, which he did very well. He did a great job on it; there was no problem. The hardest thing I remember was that you couldn't get Gibson pickup surround screws at the time, so Sam was sourcing everything from every little back street screw shop to try and find something that sort of resembled it. He'd go shooting down Lisle Street looking for old odds and sods that might have at some time been RAF spares!

With the slew of rock bands that were appearing on the scene, many of whom relied upon heavy overseas touring schedules to maintain their profiles, it was likely that Sam's skills in terms of refinishing, fixing and painting guitars damaged in transit, etc. proved invaluable. In truth, Sam Li could hardly have picked a better time in the history of music to start out on his own. His foresight was paying off.

Pete Finbow (Sam Li's friend): *I first met Sam in Gerrard Street after I'd gone into Macari's on Charing Cross Road to ask about a re-fret. Mr Macari told me to see the main man, Sam Li, and to ask him if he'd do the job. I took it to Sam, and he simply said, 'OK.' From then on I referred to him as 'one-word answer Sam'.*

One day while I was there, a guy came in looking for a new nut for his Fender. Sam said he could replace it but that it

*would be very expensive. 'How much?' the guy asked him. '£15',
Sam told him. The guy was shocked. '£15 for just a piece of
plastic?' he said. 'Ivory', Sam replied. The guy asked if he could
do it cheaper. 'Even if you fall to your knees clutching your heart,
when you get back up it'll still be £15!' Sam told him.*

Under the instruction of the various guitar stores issuing
directions to Sam's workshop, off these musicians would go,
dressed head to toe in denim perhaps, guitar case in hand -
completely oblivious to the fact that by crossing the threshold
of Sam's Gerrard Street building, they might as well be stepping
through a stargate and into a separate dimension.

Albert Lee (blues guitarist): *I had a Martin 00028
guitar that needed one of the ribs re-glued. This was probably
early 1970. I'd heard about Sam Li by reputation in the scene.
Everybody spoke well of him. So I went around to his office - this
quaint little upstairs room near Wardour Street. He was clearly
busy - there were guitar parts everywhere. I remember him being
a very nice guy and I was surprised when he complimented me
for having such a nice guitar.*

*I don't recall that he set it up. Everyone has a preference
when it comes to setup and there's a fine balance between tone
and action: too low and you lose tone. I'm sure I'd have noticed
if the action had changed after Sam had it. Needless to say, he did
a great repair on that Martin guitar. I still have it today.*

John Taylor (former road manager, now artist manager): *I
met Sam on several occasions during the late '60s and early '70s.
I specifically remember taking Ollie Halsall's white Gibson SG
up to Sam when I was the road manager for his band, Patto, in
about 1970. Nice guy.*

Peter Finbow: *Colin Cooper of the Climax Blues Band had a cherry red Gretsch that someone had somehow stood on the neck and broken it at the fifth fret. I met Colin in the Vox music store and he told me that Sam was going to fix the neck. Thereafter it would also need a colour match. Because I knew about paint at the time, I knew that Dylon - a natural pigment - was the best thing to use because, if you applied a synthetic stain and then applied cellulose on top, it bubbled. That didn't happen with Dylon. When he got the guitar back, Colin said the finish was first class.*

With a variety of guitar parts placed on available horizontal surfaces in various states of repair and the dense aroma of a combination of wood adhesive, solder and Kensitas cigarettes hanging heavy in the air, Sam Li's workshop really was a different world - a quiet, introverted world at that - and one that was at complete odds with its nonstop, bustling street environs below.

While there was a transistor radio on the table beside him, few can recall ever hearing it playing. No clock ticked and no phone rang. The only item that gave any clue to any sort of interest outside of his work was the newspaper open at that day's horseracing cards. The only audible sounds were the barely perceivable kind that you'd imagine might accompany focused work and perfectionism.

Fiona Beattie: *It was obvious that Sam liked his workshop above the Kowloon. Even I, as young as I was, could tell that. Furthermore, he would go downstairs for lunch where he'd often order Chinese pork and rice for seven shillings and sixpence in old money.*

As a young girl, I was just fascinated watching him work. I remember so vividly the ratchet screwdriver and manual drill, the smell of the wood glue, seeing clamps with various guitar parts being put together and the sight and sound of wood being planed smooth. In general, he had such high standards.

As lacquer dried on a guitar neck or while newly bedded frets were setting, Sam would frequently look out of the first floor window down to the street, which in those days was less busy, and see the next customer arriving in their newly acquired Rolls Royce - the ultimate musician status symbol that simply said: 'I've made it.'

He'd watch what he'd consider to be these young, scruffily dressed artists clamber out of their expensive motors and ascend the wooden stairs to his workshop, damaged instrument or cash in hand, depending on the situation.

As they approached, Sam Li's feelings were perhaps conflicted. On one hand, he would certainly be appreciative of all of this custom. The mortgage on his London home depended on it. But curiously, on the other, the perfectionist in him would be a little disappointed that these privileged young musicians weren't dressed immaculately, as he himself always was.

David (Sam's nephew): *I never remember him looking anything other than smart and immaculate, whatever he was doing and wherever he went. Even his hairstyle was always neat and nicely combed. One thing I always noticed was that he particularly liked Bally shoes.*

Fiona Beattie: *He liked shopping at the Swiss Centre and he was always smartly dressed. I remember once that he proudly showed me his brand new Aquascutum Crombie cashmere* *overcoat. He smiled and said, 'I won't tell you how much it cost...'*

In Sam Li's eyes, as much as the business was becoming his lifeblood, rock 'n' roll just wasn't a good look. Jeans per se were fine. But scruffy, torn denim held no attraction at all and trainers were only to be worn on a sports field.

Sam preferred smart suits, preferably the highest quality clothes from Savile Row, Simpsons of Piccadilly or Dunhill. His shoes were always polished. Sam Li's appearance was immaculate and, in keeping, his work had to meet the same exacting standards.

Edmond Leu: *Sam had this kind of way about him. It was hard to know how to take him. I think it's a quirky Guianese thing. I remember being with him once when he took a new tweed jacket he'd just bought to the tailors to have the sleeves shortened one day. The tailor just took a pair of scissors and hacked two inches off each sleeve, right in front of him. It was no doubt a very expensive jacket. Sam looked at the tailor and quietly said 'You keep the jacket' and walked out.*

Beyond their attire, Sam exhibited little by way of appreciation for the actual music many of his clients played - particularly when seeing the boisterous and somewhat uncouth image that came with it.

As a dyed-in-the wool jazzman with an almost reverential view on the sanctity of that genre, rock, blues and glam music just weren't appealing to him - although there's no doubt that he felt a degree of pride when observing their obvious success. In Sam Li's mind, on some level he was supporting, facilitating even, these musicians' endeavours.

Nevertheless, despite his personal feelings, Sam was

always professional and respectful enough not to allow his tastes to impact his work or the many relationships it brought him. If he was ever asked to comment on a client's music, he usually chose not to.

If he was ever forced into offering up a critique, his response was generally influenced by whatever mood he happened to be in at that moment. Sometimes there might be a witty retort with that stern expression and booming voice he reputedly had. Other times that implacable, withering sideways stare. And Sam Li was certainly a man of often contradictory moods.

Fiona Beattie: *He could be such a brilliant, quiet man. But at times he certainly had bad moods. On the other hand, he was so incredibly kind and thoughtful. He never forgot birthdays and always gave cards with very loving messages.*

One day in 1969 my mother, heavily pregnant, asked me to run up the road to get some groceries. She gave me £5 and told me not to lose it, as it was a lot of money. I cycled up there and, while shopping, hung on to the fiver. But somehow I lost it in the shop. I was so upset and didn't want the telling-off from my mother and decided not to go home.

I rode as far away as I could on my bicycle but became so tired that the only option was to return home hours later. I was most surprised when arriving home, my mother only asked what happened and immediately telephoned Sam saying 'She's home.' When Sam arrived home, he walked in the door carrying the biggest bag of chocolates and sweets, our favourites, and handed them to me to share with my brother. I didn't understand why at the time.

To his clients in the workplace, Sam Li often gave little away. As one customer remembers: 'He was very mysterious'. I had no background on him at all - other than from other players that also went there. On some days he'd be relatively animated, for him at least. He might have even offered me an instant coffee one time. On other days you'd get nothing from him at all. He'd just stare at you. I felt like I was in a doctor's surgery.'

Revealingly, as much as Sam valued the custom these rising stars were bringing him every day and as proud as he surely was of their success and his association with it, at no point did he ever mention his connection with any of them, far less brag about it.

Fame, per se, was not Sam Li's motivation. In fact, it was as if the stardom to which he was associated on a daily basis didn't faze him at all.

David (Sam's nephew): *Sam never ever told me exactly who his visitors and clients were. Some people would shout their head off about such things but not Sam. He kept everything to himself. I felt that his attitude was a measure of the professional respect for the people who were his customers. The truth is that many of them probably were stars.*

Fiona Beattie: *Over time, the people Sam worked with became routine for me. Sam would come home and mention these names, obviously talking to my mother about his day. It was just normal. He took everyone at face value. He used to talk about these people who were legitimately huge stars and say to me things like 'Well, they are human, they bring me their guitars for repair - they are just people.'*

One day in the early '70s, Sacha Distel made the pilgrimage to 19 Gerrard Street. Born in Paris in 1933, Distel initially pursued a career as a pianist before switching to jazz guitar. He appeared on the Ed Sullivan Show in the late 1950s and landed two big hits: 'Brigitte', homage to Brigitte Bardot released in 1958, and, later, 'La Belle Vie', released in the early 1960s.

Carrying a guitar that had a problem whereby the 2nd and 3rd strings kept breaking at inopportune moments, Distel walked into Sam Li's workshop in late 1970.

Sam took one look at the guitar and reported that the reason for the breakages was the nickel frets the previous luthier had used.

'They're wearing through the strings,' Sam said.

'OK. Can you re-fret it?' Sacha asked. 'I'm doing a duet tonight at the London Palladium with Barney Kessel.'

Sam told him that he could and turned down the extra money he was offered for the quick turnaround. And, with that knowing look, he promised Sacha that the guitar would be ready for collection at 5 p.m. that evening.

When Sacha returned at the appointed pick-up time, the two sat and chatted for a while. He told Sam the story of how he became a singer in the first place.

A group he was in was about to go on stage one night when the existing singer fell ill. Desperate, the band looked at each other for inspiration and the best idea they could apparently come up with was to ask Sacha to sing. Initially he was reluctant. But, after a bit of moaning and groaning, he agreed. With that he walked on stage, the ladies swooned and the rest is history.

Sam just loved hearing these stories. But, as interested as he was by this bizarre bunch of people, he didn't put them on anything like the same pedestal that their fans obviously did. On the contrary: he took pleasure in poking fun at them.

As Sacha was about to leave, Sam handed him the guitar and said, 'Here. Try this.'

As Sacha began playing, Sam's face changed momentarily from the trademark implacable stare to one of complete amazement.

'I can't believe you can actually play that!' Sam told him, shaking his head with wide eyes.

Sacha laughed nervously. Sam did not.

Distel left.

Another satisfied customer!

Doug Ellis: *I used to run into Sacha at lunch breaks after I'd moved to Sound City. It was perfectly normal to see people you knew wandering around Soho in those days. 'I was just coming to see you to buy a guitar case,' he said to me one day. 'Let's go back and do it,' I replied. It was such a fabulous time.*

Gordon Hawtin (session player, guitar shop employee, photographer): *I got my first actual job in a guitar shop, Sound City, on January 11ᵗʰ 1967. It was my sixteenth birthday. Within a short period of time, I met an unknown Jimi Hendrix and sold Noel Redding his jazz bass that he was famous for. I think he paid a hundred guineas for it. They took it away in the shipping box but, before they did, Noel showed me how to play 'Hey Joe' and Jimi gave me a few little tips. I attracted people. I was a bit of a mad raconteur. I used to do crazy things like nail plectrums to the floor. Then I'd watch people trying to pick them up. I got Mick Ralphs with that; I got Paul McCartney too!*

Anyway, I left Sound City and then returned there a couple of years later to work in their sister shop Modern Sound. It was here that I met Sam Li for the first time because by this time he was Sound City's guitar repairer. By this time it was common knowledge in London that he'd done that work on Peter Green's Les Paul. Everybody in the business knew. From my experience, all those people in the guitar shops in the West End loved to gossip but they didn't like putting out false gossip.

Sam was an incredibly private person. He didn't suffer fools gladly. I had this mad loon kind of a personality and he always just gave me looks. He was also very suspicious and wasn't averse to wanting something for nothing; he cultivated me a little because he knew I could put business his way - which I did.

Consequently, I went into his workshop quite often. From memory there was a big workbench that was the length of the three windows with views out the front. To the side was another bench that had a vice and various wood cutting tools on it - fancy saws that could cut around corners. I got the impression that everything he did was by hand. There weren't power tools available in those days anyway.

CHAPTER SEVEN

In 1968, the Francis Rossi-fronted Status Quo released what is now considered to be quite a psychedelic debut in the form of Pictures of Matchstick Men.

Over the following decade, with the trademark duo of lead singer/guitarist Francis Rossi and guitar player Rick Parfitt, who had joined in late 1967, 'Quo'- as they became affectionately known - settled into a straight ahead and undeniably effective boogie-rock groove, based around traditional twelve bar blues. This not only saw the band tour worldwide but also yielded many chart hits and vast album sales. For the duration of the '70s and the '80s, there were few bigger rock bands in the UK than Status Quo. 128 million album sales to date merely confirm that status.

Born in London's Forest Hill neighbourhood in 1949 to a father of Italian heritage and a mother whose descendants hailed from Northern Ireland, Francis Rossi befriended bass player Alan Lancaster while playing the trumpet in the school orchestra at Sedgehill Comprehensive.   Those two, along with a couple of other enthusiastic classmates, formed their first band, The Scorpions, in 1962 (not to be confused with the German hard rock outfit of the same name). Having played leisure centres, town halls and, ultimately, a Butlins holiday camp in 1965, the band was then renamed The Spectres. It was at Butlins in Minehead that Francis Rossi met Rick Parfitt for the first time - while Parfitt was playing in another band called The Highlights.

Thereafter, Rossi not only secured a record deal for The Spectres in 1966 but also laid the bedrock of a friendship and working partnership with Parfitt that would last many decades.

After releasing two singles as part of their five-year deal with Piccadilly records that made little by way of chart impact, Rossi's band stood at a crossroads. In 1966, psychedelic music was all the rage. Short-lived fad or not, it was sink or swim. As it turned out, Rossi swam - and changed the band's name again to Traffic Jam while also adopting a more psychedelic sound in keeping with the time.

A year later, the band's evolution was complete when Rossi wrote the track 'Pictures of Matchstick Men' while changing the band's name for the final time, to Status Quo. Simultaneously, Parfitt cemented his friendship with Rossi by joining his band. The rest, as they say, is history.

Francis Rossi: *I think it was someone in Sound City that first told me about Sam. This was probably '67, '68 or '69. I also heard about him from a member of Thin Lizzy or such like. Anyway, somebody would have said, 'Try Sam Li. He's your man.' I'd go there – I think in those days you could park somewhere nearby. Then I'd walk to his place with my guitar. And I liked that I could walk up, leave it and then go back in an hour or whatever it was. As I got to know him, we'd have a cup of tea and a chinwag. I really grew to like him.*

He understood Fender guitars and it was an intonation issue that I first went to him about. Because the bridges that used to be on Telecasters are almost like a three-seat bridge, if you wanted to tune the intonation at the top between the bridge and the top of the neck, that's where you did it. If you wanted to do the second string but you didn't want to move the first, you couldn't do anything because of the way Teles were designed where two strings each shared one of the straight-bar bridge saddles.

Sam in Selmer cubbyhole
testing guitar
Circa 1960

Sam in Gerrard Street
workShop
Early 1970's

Pictured top: Sam with Dick Cheung outside flat in Princes Square
September 1960

Pictured bottom: Sam with his band in Hyde Park
Circa 1960

Pictured top: Jack Parnell and his band

Pictured bottom Left: Sam with his guitar *circa 1960*

Pictured bottom right: Sam when he first arrived in London *1959*

Pictured bottom: Steve Howe, Doug Ellis & Bruce Bolen

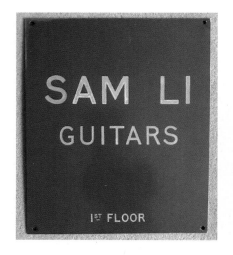

Pictured top left: The sign from Sam's workshop

Pictured top right: Sam working in his workshop *Circa 1970*

Pictured middle left: "The Sam Li Flying V made for Tommy Willis and now owned by Fiona Beattie. With just one Gibson humbucker

Pictured opposite - middle right : The guitar made by Sam Li which was reputedly used by Allan Holdsworth, Jeff Beck and Jeff Lynne.

Pictured opposite - bottom: The now famous hit-maker guitar made by Sam Li and bought from Sound City Music Store by Slade's Dave Hill

Pictured top left: The original neck colour of the guitar played by Allan Holdsworth is just visible in the truss rod compartment

Pictured top middle & Right: The cable compartment shows the fine wiring job, using shielded coax cable with multiple grounding points

Pictured bottom left: Sam Li's preferred Schaller tuners, made in W.Germany at that time.

Pictured bottom middle: The two humbucker pickups. On the left, the neck pickup - Gibson with patent number. On the right, the bridge pickup, probably of Japanese origin given the offset holes and wiring

Pictured bottom right: Sam Li's 'Custom Made' identifier in front of the neck pickup." Photo credits Paul Higgins

Pictured top: Sam and Babs *1961*

Pictured middle: Sam with Fiona *1962*

Pictured Bottom: Sam with his daughter Laura *1970*

Seasons
Greetings
from the
BAY CITY ROLLERS
ROAD CREW
(jake)

Hi Sam -
I'm at the Isle of
Skye for a week but
will be back to say
hello before leaving
for Germany. Take
care and see you soon
Seymour

205-9846

Sam Li
36 Ross Lyn Hill
Hamstead
London, Eng.
N.W.3.

Pictured top: Sam visiting his niece Mooi in USA *Circa 1990*

Pictured middle: Sam playing piano with friend in USA *Circa 1990*

Pictured right: Christmas card from Bay City Rollers road crew

Pictued bottom left: Postcard from Seymour Duncan.

Francis Rossi - Status Quo *"Sam Li, the only man who knew my guitar better than I did"*

Pictured above left : Kirk Hammett - Metallica pictured with 'Greeny' Image provided by Ross Halfin

Pictured above right: Dave Hill - Slade playing one of Sam's guitars

So I asked Sam about it and he said he used to use a Gibson, which had a bridge with six saddles on it, so you could do the intonation the way I wanted. He then switched the saddles over for me for a tilt-compensated saddle that permitted correct intonation. Thereafter, whatever Sam suggested, I did it. If I ever thought 'Ah fuck it, I don't know what's wrong with it', I'd just take it to Sam's. And he would say 'Ah, you bloody idiot, this is wrong or that's wrong' or 'this is what you do'. He never failed me.

Eric Bell (Thin Lizzy): *It wasn't me that Francis spoke to! My best guess is that it would have been Gary Moore...*

Francis Rossi: *Sam got me through a lot with my guitars. Everyone always talks about my green Telecaster but I don't think it was green when I had it with Sam. I had had this guitar since about '68 and, for some reason, I thought I'd sand it down to the wood. So I did it at home with discs and thought it looked nice and then, being young, I thought I'd paint it black. I painted it, took it to a gig and then it dried out to this horrible grey colour. I didn't want to play it looking like that. Then I think I sanded it down again and painted it with Ronseal because, with it, you could paint wood and still see the grain. On the day that I was doing it, I suddenly looked at the watch and realised I had a gig and had to put the guitar back together again. I don't think it was even finished. People got very silly about that guitar. It became the famous green Telecaster.*

He did some electrical stuff with my Telecaster too. Teles, being single-coil pickups, tend to pick up all kinds of shit in the air. And then they start buzzing and doing all sorts of other things. Sam was the first person who taught me that where the volume control, the toggle switch and the tone control are, there's also this gully into which he slotted a piece of silver paper. Thereafter, all the problems were sorted!

Nowadays, when I have a problem with a guitar and I give it to someone who procrastinates, I never quite trust what's been done. That was never a thought with Sam. I picked up a guitar from him, took it to a gig and played it. And of course it was fine because Sam had done it.

While obviously focused specifically on Sam Li's skills, some of Rossi's comments clearly allude to some broader cultural differences that clearly separate today from, for example, the 1970s.

It would certainly seem Sam Li's era was far less driven by commercialism and consumerism. If something broke, people existed specifically to fix it whereas nowadays, without wishing to over-generalise, if something falls into disrepair, somebody often just buys a new item.

Consequently, the relationship between the customer and the people whose craftsmanship skills have been developed over time specifically to service them is less common.

Francis Rossi: *I don't think people like Sam are around anymore. He seemed to be able to develop with me - and other people, I assume - a relationship whereby he learned to understand exactly what that individual needed. I really miss having Sam there. There was such a great vibe associated with that whole idea of 'Take it to Sam…'.*

Phil Harris: *I saw a lot of guitars in there at various times. Dave Hill's guitar was in there. Status Quo's guitars were in there. In fact, Sam told me that the reason Francis Rossi's green guitar had a hole drilled through it was that, if someone ever* stole it, they'd never be able to fill the hole convincingly. If it ever showed up re-sprayed or plugged, it would also be identifiable. Sam also told me he worked on Rick Parfitt's guitar - put the Gibson tailpiece on it and all that.

Pete Cornish: *All these guitars became like old friends to me. Francis Rossi's green Telecaster came to me many times for electrical work. On one occasion, Sam came into Sound City with this look of great terror on his face. We made him tea and, after a bit of calming down, he related a tale about how he was cutting a pickup recess in a guitar body when the router fell out while still rotating at high speed. Seemingly it went straight through the guitar body, through the workbench, between his legs and then ended up embedded in the floor! Whether that's what put the hole in that green Telecaster, who knows?*

Given Status Quo's simple but appealing formula, it's of little surprise that the relationship between Sam and Rossi represented something of a musical culture clash. While Sam undoubtedly thought highly of Rossi the man on a personal level, Status Quo's music seemingly didn't do it for him at all...

Francis Rossi: *He must have known I wasn't a particularly accomplished player but he never treated me any differently than all the other serious players that used to go to him. He never made me feel uncomfortable or else I couldn't have gone to him. He always made me feel fine as if to say 'No, you're as valid as any other customer that I have here'. There was a lot of that kind of snobbery around music at that time but not from Sam. Sam never struck me as one of those jazz types who was a snob about rock music, pop music or blues. I never actually knew he was a jazz muse at the time anyway. I just thought he was an all-*

rounder. But I know jazzers are really good. I was his customer and, as such, he always treated me with the utmost respect. I was proud to have him as my friend.

Fiona Beattie: *I later heard that Francis Rossi once invited Sam to a Quo gig. Sam went with his friend Pete Finbow and, after the gig, when talking to the band, Francis said to Sam 'So you came then?' and asked Sam what he thought of the gig. 'Loud' was Sam's reply!*

Edmond Leu: *I saw lots of people in there at various times. I saw Francis Rossi in there. Sam joked with him that his guitar skills were a bit average! Another time someone came in to collect a guitar for Elton John. And then on another occasion Rod Stewart came in to collect a guitar and Sam laughed and said to him: 'You can't sing. You have a hoarse voice!'*

* * *

Taking their name from the town Nazareth, Pennsylvania, which was cited in the song 'The Weight' by The Band, the rock band Nazareth was founded in 1968 in Dunfermline, Scotland out of the remnants of two local semi-professional acts called The Shadettes and The Red Hawks.

Having moved to London in 1970 to pursue a recording career, Nazareth, their self-titled debut album, was released in 1971. The band had continued success throughout the seventies and early eighties. Although, as is common with many bands of the time, line-up changes, combined with the ever-changing fabric of the music world, saw the band's fortunes decline somewhat in the 1980s.

That said, a version of the band continued to tour and

release music and is still active today. Dundee-born bass player Pete Agnew is the only remaining founding member still playing in Nazareth today.

Pete Agnew (Nazareth): *We first came across Sam when we were recording our first album at Trident Studios in London. We needed one of the guitars repaired (can't remember which one or why) and the resident engineer at Trident, the now very well-known Roy Thomas Baker, who produced Queen etc., recommended that our roadie, Wullie, take it round the corner to a guy he had heard some of the musicians at Trident mentioning as being very good with guitars. That person turned out to be Sam Li.*

The guitar was repaired and, during that first visit, Wullie told Sam that we were looking for an acoustic guitar to record one of the tracks and Sam told him about one he had just worked on and that it was now up for sale in a shop in Tottenham Court Rd. It was a little Martin guitar that we ended up buying and using on umpteen albums throughout our career.

Another thing Sam did at my request was to fit a Fender Precision neck onto my very first bass, which was a Fender Mustang. The Mustang was a short scale model and I loved the body size but always fancied a longer neck. It's not as simple as it sounds - you can't just whip off one and screw on another. It needs a lot of fine adjustments and it was the first time (and might have been the only time) that Sam had been asked to do this.

Needless to say, he did a cracking job and I used that guitar on almost every hit record Nazareth had right up until I switched to using an Alembic, which I still play today. That Mustang has pride of place as an exhibit in the Carnegie Library & Galleries in my hometown of Dunfermline (it's the first thing you see when you enter the Galleries), so you could say that it's as much Sam's work on show as it is a compliment to mine.

Sam became 'the man to go to' for our road crew any time we had work on guitars needing done in those early days and the same was the case with most of our pals in other bands in London.

You would hear his name mentioned often either backstage or in the pubs/clubs that the bands congregated in. You'd always overhear roadies saying '...and took it round to Sam...blah, blah, blah' - that kind of thing. He was a well-loved and respected man and the rock world is a better place for having had him around.

One of the enduring memories of Fiona Beattie's childhood was seeing correspondence from the various artists that her stepfather was connected to. Cards, gifts and their latest album releases were seemingly commonplace in the family home to the extent that Sam had almost become a member of these bands' extended families.

Pete Agnew: *I know he did a lot of stuff for us over the years and we certainly didn't send Christmas cards to just anybody, so he was regarded as a friend of the band.*

* * *

Given his escalating reputation by the early '70s there was a better-than-average chance that most important repair jobs would ultimately fall into Sam's hands; it thereby felt as if iconic guitars - specifically Les Paul guitars - followed Sam Li around.

It was 1968 when Hampstead-born guitarist Paul Kossoff first teamed up with singer Paul Rodgers, drummer Simon Kirke and bass player Andy Fraser to form the blues-rock band Free.

While their debut, Tons of Sobs, and the follow-up a

year later entitled, simply, Free, gently introduced the band to a growing worldwide audience, it was their third album, Fire and Water, released in 1970, that really broke the band on a major scale.

Gordon Hawtin: *The first time I ever met Paul Kossoff was in 1965 when I went into Selmer. I was just fourteen. Unknown to me at that time, Sam Li worked there alongside another great Indian jazz musician called Amancio de Silva. Kossoff was a salesman - and a f*cking arrogant little kid he was too. I already knew of him from growing up in Hampstead.*

Free seemingly had it all. In Rodgers, they had a charismatic frontman with a gritty yet soulful rock voice. In Kossoff they had a moody and slightly mysterious gunslinger of a guitarist. The two complemented each other perfectly and the track 'All Right Now' remains a classic rock radio mainstay to this day.

However, after playing Isle of Wight in 1970 to rave critical reviews and touring worldwide, Free split up for the first time late in 1970. The death of Kossoff's hero, Jimi Hendrix, and his own spiralling drug dependency issues are generally cited as the primary reasons.

Doug Ellis: *I also previously knew Paul Kossoff as a schoolboy who would often come in with his famous father to try guitars. His father, David, who was very well-known at the time, was an actor and broadcaster. He was an absolute gentleman. He learned my name and was invariably courteous, charming and good humoured with an endearing humility. He made a lasting impression on me. I would have been about twenty years old.*

By 1972 the band had reformed and were touring the UK, in part it was rumoured, in an attempt to distract Kossoff from his heroin addiction. On the last night of the tour at the Mayfair Ballroom in Newcastle, Kossoff's guitar, another '59 Les Paul Standard variant, was thrown up in the air only to land straight down on the headstock. The force of the impact was transmitted down the guitar, shearing the neck on or around the fifth fret.

Steve Clarke: *The repair on the midsection, from around the fifth fret up to the headstock, was done by Sam Li during late 1972 and the first several months of 1973. Arthur Ramm, who now owns the guitar and whose band - Beckett - was supporting Free that night, related the story to me himself. He knew Kossoff well and he'd loaned him a guitar, a 1968 Gold Top Les Paul refinished in sunburst, to finish the Newcastle show. According to Arthur, Kossoff's Les Paul sat in Sam Li's workshop on Gerrard Street for quite some time, presumably in line behind a number of other repairs, even though I'm sure Kossoff wanted it back as soon as possible.*

Having seen it, I can confirm that it's a very, very good repair. It's a different piece of mahogany that's been used; the grain is slightly different. From there everything else was rebuilt. One thing I noticed was a familiar luthier's trick. To cut down on drying time (lacquer can take many weeks to dry out fully) I think Sam tried to save time by putting some masking tape over the Gibson logo on the headstock. This is in no way a reflection of his workmanship but I think he needed to save time by spraying around the tape. The problem is, he hadn't levelled it first, so there's a rectangular mark left there. I just don't think he had the time. But in general his inlay work and woodwork was absolutely stunning. The new binding that was put on up near the nut was absolutely as good as what Gibson would have done.

As the story goes, Sam finished the repair job sometime in the latter part of 1973 whereupon Kossoff came to Gerrard Street and collected the guitar, despite having done a deal with Ramm to swap it for the '68 Gold Top he'd been loaned in Newcastle. The guitar then passed through various other hands including, it is said, those of Roxy Music's guitarist Phil Manzanera.

Edmond Leu: *I saw broken guitars that Sam had put back together so well that you couldn't even see the break. I heard many artists say that his repair work was just great.*

Fiona Beattie: *If something was damaged, he would no longer be interested in that item if it could not be repaired perfectly. Ironically, he was never very good at DIY at home. He would start a job in the house, like decorating the bathroom or removing the kitchen tiles off the walls in preparation, but the job would never get finished. Perhaps he didn't have time?*

Doug Ellis: *While I was working in Sound City, I remember Sam coming in one day and being disgruntled about a DIY job he was doing at home. He was bemoaning the fact that he had spent the weekend decorating a room. I think he had started to wallpaper the room and found that the walls weren't quite square or true. If I or anyone else had been doing it, they'd have overlapped the edges of the wallpaper or painted it or something. Not Sam. He went out and bought bags of plaster and plastered the room square! This took him all weekend!*

Tragically, Paul Kossoff died on a flight from Los Angeles to New York in March 1976 as a result of a blood clot caused by a pulmonary embolism.

Doug Ellis: *The last time I saw Paul he was very confused and rather aggressive. He recognised me and shouted a bit. It was all very sad and a complete waste of a formidable talent. His death would have broken his father's heart.*

Once again, a valuable and iconic guitar had passed through Sam Li's artful hands and had outlived one of its best-known owners. Perhaps fairly, an agreement was reached between Kossoff's girlfriend, Sandie Chard, and Arthur Ramm some time after Kossoff's death.

The swap agreement was honoured and Arthur Ramm owned and gigged the '59 Les Paul used on iconic hits like 'All Right Now' right up until 2015, when the guitar was advertised for sale at Bonham's auctioneers. The guitar rumour mill says that bids reached £130,000 before the auction was halted and the guitar withdrawn, having failed to reach the reserve.

Phil Harris: *I could have bought that guitar out of the Orange guitar shop in 1974! It was in there for £450, but I didn't want it because of the repair to the neck. In those days, there weren't guitar collectors anyway. A vintage guitar was just an old guitar. We were guitar players, first and foremost.*

For that reason, I didn't buy it and it then went back to Paul Kossof because, when they realised that he had sold the guitar to pay for heroin, management bought it. He died of heroin in the end, of course, but, at the time, they bought the guitar back to give back to him because he'd sold every other guitar he had to pay for drugs. When he died, Arthur Ramm eventually got it and he brought it over to a guitar show at Haydock Park a few years ago where I finally got the opportunity to play it.

CHAPTER EIGHT

Having first supported Deep Purple in 1970, Ritchie Blackmore - who reputedly had fret work on his own trademark Fender Stratocaster carried out at some point by Sam Li - was so impressed by Wishbone Ash that he recommended them to the producer Derek Lawrence. At the same time, Blackmore helped the band negotiate a record deal with the MCA/Decca record label.

On the back of their breakthrough third album, Argus, released in 1973, Wishbone Ash became a legitimate headline act playing arenas worldwide.

In 1974, the band temporarily relocated to the US. Commercial success stayed with the band towards the end of that decade until fall-outs resulting in enforced line-up changes stalled their progress somewhat.

Andy Powell (Wishbone Ash): *For the first year or two of playing in Wishbone Ash, I used a homemade guitar. Predictably, I was never out of wood shops, getting things fixed. Eventually I needed somebody reliable to do repairs; guitars were regularly getting damaged because flight cases didn't exist in the early '70s. On at least one occasion, when I came back from a trip, I had the headstock completely broken off a guitar. Things happened on tour; we were all just learning the art of putting on a rock show. Racks for guitars weren't available; guitar techs didn't exist either. And so road managers would regularly trip over the guitars or they'd get dropped somewhere. So from memory it was*

Mick Ralphs of Bad Company that recommended Sam to me. And I'm pretty sure I would have gravitated to someone like Sam because guitars were always very precious to me. Later, other band members also went to him.

Thereafter, I started enjoying the simple act of going into Soho - even taking time out to go down there on the tube felt good. It was all so new and exciting. If it were just a simple job, I'd leave it with him and go down and buy some kind of exotic Chinese takeaway, just because I could. And the very fact that you could buy a proper Italian coffee appealed to me. Then maybe I'd wander around and get a feel for all the various little stores before going back to pick up the guitar. It was a day out.

Laurie Wisefield (Wishbone Ash and Home, session guitar player for Tina Turner and Joe Cocker): *I think I heard about Sam via the marvellous Jerry Donahue. Although I didn't know Jerry personally, he was connected with a lot of my contemporaries that I really respected, like Albert Lee and Ray Smith from Heads Hands & Feet, who I was a big fan of.*

I remember Sam's workshop as being this small room in Chinatown upstairs. It was nothing remarkable - just this small space, a little funky as Gerrard Street generally was in those days, with a bench I think in front of the window and a load of bits/ pieces and tools spread around.

What was clearer was the fact that Sam seemed a bit grumpy on first meeting! I was a young kid, probably only in my twenties, pretty green and wet behind the ears, not knowing much about guitars, how they worked or how to set them up. Sam clearly sensed this, as it was fairly obvious, and I remember his slightly grumpy attitude with me on that day where he was probably thinking 'oh here we go... another kid who don't know shit!'

From memory, the guitar I took to Sam, probably in 1971, to work on was a blond Fender Telecaster - which wasn't a very good one and was later swapped for a 1966 Strat that had been sanded down to the wood. That deal was done in one of the shops in Denmark Street sometime after and they told me in the shop that the Strat had previously belonged to Richard Thompson. Not sure if that was true or they were just giving me some spiel! I liked the Strat though and kept it for a while.

Anyway, Sam picked up my Telecaster and started playing a jazz tune with all the melody in chords. Never in my life had I really seen anyone do that before, especially close up. I remember feeling quite intimidated by it as I could see that he clearly had a knowledge that I didn't have of the instrument. Looking back, it's in those moments that you get a small inkling of something that helps you further down the line. Sam was a fabulous chord player - old school jazz style.

When I joined the band Home with Mick Stubbs and Cliff Williams in 1971, it turned out that Mick had a custom-made guitar that had been built by Sam Li. From memory, it was a cherry red SG shape. It was a double cutaway and I think it may have had a couple of extra switches added that possibly switched the pickups in/out of phase. I remember vividly when Mick got it and was playing it as we rehearsed in a room in Kings Cross before recording our first album. I think a lot of tracks from the first Home album, Pause for a Hoarse Horse, were recorded with Mick Stubbs playing that guitar.

Andy Powell: *His place was on an upper level above a takeaway. There was a door to the side and you'd go up the stairs to a tiny little room with a workbench and a radio on a nearby table. No assistant, no apprentice, just him. It was immediately obvious that he knew what he was doing. The initial repairs he* *did for me were not only done correctly but they were also done to a higher standard than I actually required.*

I became attracted to his inscrutable nature. I never had any idea what he was thinking. Did he think I was an idiot? Did he think rock music was cool? I'll never know. But that intrigued me, and I kept going back for more, and we did reach a level of friendship whereby he occasionally would get his guitar out and play me a few chords.

Predictably perhaps, Wishbone Ash's rising stock did little to impress Sam Li. If anything, it seemed as if he looked upon typical rock star antics, shenanigans whereby valuable instruments got broken, with a degree of disappointed disdain. After all, Sam was a craftsman. To him, regardless of the client's status, the integrity of the craft meant much more than some of the more superficial aspects of devil-may-care rock 'n' roll.

Andy Powell: *If I could hang out with Sam more than the allotted time, I always would. Sometimes he'd even offer me a cup of coffee but he was always quite a stern character.*

As time passed, I found ways of sweet-talking him, acting pathetic in the hope that he'd accommodate my guitar in the long list of instruments he had waiting to be repaired. While I managed this a few times, he always had this way of looking at you sideways as if to say: 'You silly bugger. How did you manage to do that?' I always felt kind of guilty. I'd often go in there with my tail between my legs!

Martin Turner (Wishbone Ash): *Sam repaired a badly broken Gibson Thunderbird for me, which I acquired from Pete Watts of Mott the Hoople, who, by his own admission, had abused the instrument. It required a new headstock to be made* *and grafted into the neck that Sam clearly thought long and hard about. He also gave me a fairly lengthy interview in which I felt he wanted to find out if he even liked me enough to do the repair. I guess I passed the test and he repaired the guitar in about 1973 I think. He recommended a re-spray mainly to hide the cracks and dings so I opted for an Ivory colour although I had never seen a Thunderbird in that colour prior to that time.*

I used the instrument as my main stage bass throughout the '70s, '80s and since performing - predominantly with Wishbone Ash. His repair failed just a few years ago when it was stuffed in the overhead on a flight back from Japan. Arguably, it was unwise of me to carry it in such a manner. It has been repaired again since but I have now taken to using customised, cheaper Epiphone copies - which serve me well for live appearances. I remember Sam as being sincere and somewhat serious during my dealings with him and he was undoubtedly an honest and skilled craftsman when it came to instruments. Being a young punk back then, I found meeting him a bit daunting - he was a legendary guitar man - but once I got over my initial nervousness, I really did like him and was very pleased and proud that he had done such a great repair for me.

CHAPTER NINE

While repairs and setup undoubtedly represented the bulk of Sam Li's cash flow in the early days of being self-employed on Gerrard Street, it seems likely that there was another more creative side to his personality that was seeking an outlet - even if only as a sideline occupation.

In Guiana, as we know, he had the reputation for having made exceptionally well-made furniture with no shortage of his own, unique creative flair. In time, Sam Li would be building guitars from scratch.

The correct term for someone who builds guitars has always been thought to be 'luthier.' Derived from the French word luth, meaning 'lute,' a luthier by definition is a person who constructs stringed instruments that consist of a neck and a sound-amplifying box of some kind.

Strictly speaking, however, these instruments need not necessarily be guitars. All manner of other instruments - violins, violas and other instruments played by bow rather than hand - have often been considered the domain of the luthier, certainly in the earliest days of instrument making.

During the 19th century, a separation of sorts occurred whereby guitar making - although still considered to be one of a luthier's skills - became a more distinct discipline. Several luthiers played a role in developing guitars as we know them today. An Austrian, Johann Georg Stauffer, was responsible for the development of many aspects of guitar construction: bridge pins, machine heads, etc. - as well as creating oval shaped guitar bodies with double backs.

Meanwhile, in Germany, Christian Frederick Martin, who, like Sam Li, had trained as a cabinet-maker, was making great strides himself. After a dispute between the Cabinet Maker's Guild, of which he was an active member, and the Violin Maker's Guild, Martin relocated to the US and rented a workshop in New York where he continued with his quest to develop what we now recognise as the flattop acoustic guitar. Later, the C.F Martin & Company brand was created and it still exists today under the name Martin.

In 19th century Spain, another influential luthier living in Seville, Antonio de Torres Jurado, was busy developing what we recognise today as the classical guitar. As a result of much experimentation, Torres' work zeroed in on the fact that an effective soundboard was key to the actual volume of sound that could be produced by a classical guitar.

To increase volume, Torres built guitars with not only bigger soundboards but also lighter ones made of European spruce that were arched in two directions and supported by struts to make the overall construction more robust.

Given the significance of this breakthrough, Torres' various developments were, perhaps understandably, much imitated in the years following his death in 1892. While classical guitar making has developed markedly since Torres' days, elements of his strut-bracing ideas are still used in classical guitar manufacture today.

Orville Gibson's development of mandolins and, later, the first arch-top guitars - a hollow semi-acoustic guitar with a distinctive arched (as opposed to flat) top - was perhaps the next significant development in guitar making history. Lloyd Loar, a designer working for the Gibson Company, then took Orville Gibson's work forward after the great man's death in 1918.

The culmination of Loar's work was the launch of the Gibson L5 in 1922 - often considered to be the flagship guitar of the big band era. Initially it was only offered in acoustic form, with electric variants not released until the 1940s. Variants of the L5 are still manufactured today - yet it's the early Loar variants that are most sought after by the aficionados and collectors.

New York-based luthiers John D'Angelico and Jimmy D'Aquisto both played an important role in early 20th century guitar development, before Leo Fender and Gibson/Les Paul led the way in the development of solid body electric guitars for the remainder of the 20th century and beyond. By this point it would be fair to say that these men were now guitar makers as opposed to luthiers - so far had the industry come from its early 19th century roots.

Guitar making, therefore - certainly the structural aspect of their wooden construction - fell within Sam Li's range of expertise. As such, in conjunction with regular repair and setup work, manufacture of custom instruments to client specification seemed like a logical next step for Sam Li given the direction the music world was heading.

In fact, by the time that Sam had moved his operations into the workshop above the Kowloon, he may have already built at least one guitar from scratch - a solid-bodied, natural finished beauty with a single Gibson humbucker at the neck position. While it has all the hallmarks of a prototype, Sam Li's first effort at a custom guitar showed not only much promise but also hinted at what might follow later down the line.

What seems likely is that there were many more Sam Li custom-made guitars built than was first thought. Even today, it's entirely likely that not all of his custom-made guitars have been found.

As such, nobody really knows whether a guitar Allan

Holdsworth used on his band Tempest's album, released in 1973, was made for him by Sam Li in his latter days at Gerrard Street or whether Holdsworth, who bought and sold more than his fair share of guitars throughout his life, had acquired it from either a third party or from a guitar shop. Given that Holdsworth passed away in 2017, the precise details of how he came to own a Sam Li Custom guitar might never be uncovered.

Born in Bradford in 1946, Holdsworth is considered to be one of music's most innovative guitar players with a career that spanned every genre you can think of, all of it characterised by his unique brand of legato soloing, born out of an early love of the saxophone. Few people found more ways to express themselves on the instrument than Holdsworth.

Despite his reputation among purists as something of a trailblazer, Holdsworth generally struggled to achieve sustainable commercial success, with the result being that he was often forced to sell guitars (and he used many) to make ends meet.

Denny Bridges (musician, former engineer at Air Studios): *Allan Holdsworth owned the Sam Li made custom guitar and I know that because he used it on the Tempest album he was doing with John Hiseman. I was the house engineer on the record. Then, when Allan started using John Birch guitars, there must have been a conversation between Allan and I and I ended up buying it from him. There was so much to like about the guitar - not least the sound, which was really bright and powerful - very present.*

The guitar in question is an extremely impressive piece of Sam Li craftsmanship. It's essentially a Les Paul body shape, with a single cutaway, made from solid mahogany in what appears to be a rusty brown colour. The colour of mahogany guitar bodies tends to vary and a grain-filler is also used to fill the pores in the wood before a clear coat of lacquer can be applied. It is, apparently, a very heavy guitar with a sixties feel.

Denny Bridges: *Being the house engineer at Air Studios, once I bought it, the guitar basically just stayed in the studio because in those days some of the engineers and maintenance guys would jam in the early hours of the morning when the sessions had ended. Some of us were aspiring songwriters, so a few of us would try and do a few compositions in our spare time. It was a wonderful time in music.*

Someone would often say 'Anybody got a guitar I can use?' and I would say 'As a matter of fact I do'. Consequently, various musicians played the Sam Li guitar because it was there in the studio. And it was used on a lot of records. Jeff Beck used it on the album Blow by Blow, released in 1974. I have a distinct memory of this because I was very alert to the fact that Jeff had a Fender Champ amplifier, which was 110 volts, with a British plug on the end of it. I was very concerned that someone would come along and plug it into 240-volt mains.

So I remember being in Studio 4 of the old Air Studios in Oxford Circus with that amp and the Sam Li guitar in a little overdub booth. I can picture him playing it now. Whether the recordings that he made with it actually ended up on the record, I don't know. It just wasn't cool to be taking photographs in studios back then. We wouldn't have even thought about doing it. Air Studio was a very professional environment. But Jeff Beck played the guitar and liked it.

With no significant markings other than Sam Li's 'custom' tag, which closely resembles those on other guitars he made (some of his other guitars were marked 'Sam Li'), it's hard to date this particular guitar. However, with some closer inspection of some of the guitar's features, it's possible to speculate, albeit broadly, as to when Sam might have made this instrument.

The two pickups appear to be stock, patent-numbered Gibson humbuckers; the controls are Gibson reflector knobs and the bridge is a Gibson ABR-1 variant with the retainer wire. These Tune-o-matic bridges were the later variant of the ABR-1 and, as such, were manufactured between 1962 and 1975.

The scratchboard appears to be from a Gibson jazz-style guitar and it has been reshaped to fit in this instance. The pickups are now Schallers, made in West Germany, although it's possible that these are replacements that have been added since the guitar was made.

The part of the guitar that is perhaps most revealing is the distinctive tailpiece. This particular tailpiece is from a Gibson ES-175, and was fitted to only top-of-the-range guitars in around 1958.

As many people know, this particular model of Gibson guitar is synonymous with Yes guitarist Steve Howe, so perhaps it stands to reason that this Sam Li guitar was made sometime after the two first met in Gerrard Street - perhaps in 1970 - but obviously before it was used in Air Studios in 1973 and 1974.

Denny Bridges: *You could absolutely recognise that this was an instrument of extremely high quality in terms of craftsmanship. What's more, other people around the studio at the time recognised the quality also. Mick Ralphs, who was playing on an album with Ian Hunter at the time, said on more than one occasion that he wanted it. He drooled over it but never bought it.*

Similarly, Jeff Lynne played it during the recording of ELO's On the Third Day. I have a pretty clear recollection of him playing it on 'Ma-Ma-Ma-Belle.' Again, whether those takes ended up on the album or whether he did them at another time with his Les Paul, I don't know. But he definitely played it. I later did an album with the band Stackridge, called Mr Mick, in 1976 and I know for sure that Andy Davis used the guitar on two songs: 'Steam Radio Song' and 'Fish in a Glass.'

Paul Higgins (sound engineer and current owner of Allan Holdsworth's guitar): *I was a tech and soundman for a German band called Nektar who moved to the US in 1976. I then went on to work at the House of Music in West Orange NJ (where I met Denny Bridges). I worked first as a tech, then engineer and eventually Engineer/Producer. I worked on quite a few gold albums for artists in the USA and won a Grammy for a Jimmy Cliff album, Cliffhanger, in '86. Now I am partner in an Audiovisual Integration Company. Somewhere along the line, Denny offered to sell me the guitar.*

I hadn't heard of Sam Li when I first saw it. The only other custom-made guitars I had encountered were the John Birch guitars that were made for Nektar. They had a twelve and a six string double guitar and an eight and four string double-neck bass custom, both identically finished. As amazing as they looked when they played them on stage, it was usually just one song at a time as they weighed a ton and they were a prog rock band playing fifteen minute plus songs. The Sam Li custom weighs a beefy 9lbs too. So it too demands a wide strap if played for a long time. One thing's for sure, it screams like a banshee - as Denny once told me it did!

Given all of this speculation - and it is only speculation - it seems likely that the guitar was made by Sam Li sometime around 1971 or '72 given that we know that Jeff Lynne used it on an album that was cut during the latter part of 1973.

Regardless, Sam was clearly identifying a burgeoning market whereby musicians were realising that a hand crafted instrument offered something more attractive than their off-the-shelf factory made equivalents.

With his ability to source parts via his connections with the various guitar shops combined with his enduring desire to produce high quality products, custom guitars were becoming a more than viable sideline to his buoyant repair business.

As much as Sam liked to keep his professional and private lives separate, there was inevitably some overlap. It's therefore possible that Sam Li brought private jobs home in his latter days at Selmer and thereafter.

Fiona Beattie: *I have only vague memories of Sam doing work on guitars in the house. Again, it's the smell of glue that I recall most. In fact, there were times when he would let struggling artists stay in the house while he repaired their guitar. There was one young artist that visited Sam once with a broken guitar and no money. Without a guitar, he couldn't earn so he asked Sam if he'd consider repairing the guitar and, when he found work, he'd settle the bill. Sam, of course, agreed and the guy went on to become a successful and well-known musician!*

* * *

Formed in the Wolverhampton area in 1966, the band that we now know as Slade evolved via a number of names and line-up changes which culminated in the release of a debut album entitled Beginnings in May of 1969.

Born in Devon in 1946, the son of a mechanic, Dave Hill moved to the Black Country with his parents when he was just a year or two old. Having bought his first guitar from a mail order catalogue while still at the secondary school where he received a few guitar lessons from a science teacher, Hill formed his first band, The Young Ones, while still at school.

Dave Hill (Slade): *Although I liked Buddy Holly, Elvis, Chuck Berry, Duane Eddy, Cliff Richard and the Shadows and then, of course, the Beatles, my main influence in music from a playing perspective was always skiffle - which led to the purchase of my first guitar, which was an acoustic from Kay's catalogue that cost £7.50. Let's just say that it was not good but I wanted to play it nevertheless. Thereafter, I moved on to a Burns electric Wild Dog version.*

Later, having played in local bands while also working in the offices of Tarmac Ltd in nearby Solihull, Hill met singer Noddy Holder and bass player Jimmy Lea. Slade was born.

Throughout his years in Slade - a glam rock institution if ever there was one - Hill pushed the stage image that was known as 'Yob.' This involved outrageous outfits, outlandish stage antics and, predictably, suitably off-the-wall guitars as part of the overall look.

Two guitars epitomised Dave Hill's career in Slade. The first is the 'Superyob' itself, a John Birch guitar made for him in 1973. The second is a custom Gibson-style guitar made by Sam Li in 1968, but not specifically for Dave Hill. Who Sam actually made it for is unclear. Why he made such a unique guitar at all is also a mystery. But one way or another, it found its way into Dave Hill's hands, and it would thereafter be a Slade mainstay that was present on almost all of the band's many hit records.

Dave Hill: *My manager at the time, Chas Chandler, wanted me to get a better guitar for Slade. He didn't like my Burns Wild Dog. So what happened was I was at Sound City Music Store in Shaftsbury Avenue near Soho and there it was: a Gibson-looking guitar in the window. I guess people might say it said 'Buy me'. I asked the man in there to keep it for me, and it turned out to be a one-off made by Sam Li, and the price I remember was £220, which was a lot of money at the time.*

So I went home, told my dad about it, and he drove me to London with my friend and Slade drummer Don Powell, and he bought it cash for me. It was the best investment he ever made in me and, as a tribute to my Dad, I've always referred to it as "Dad's Guitar."

So you see, Sam didn't make it for me but, in a way, it was meant for me. It was played and used because of its sound on all of the major Slade hits including the famous Christmas song. When I play that guitar, you can hear those records; it was pivotal and the most important guitar of my life. The sound was - and still is - biting, clear and rocking... It has a special tone.

The guitar in question has become well-known to guitar aficionados. While there are elements of a Gibson SG shape in Sam Li's custom Gibson-style guitar, there are also some other unusual nuances and enhancements that make this Glam rock legend of an instrument really stand out.

Dave Hill: *The standard of Sam's work was very high. I know a lot of people knew him. I guess he was gifted and did things properly - he must have done to have his guitars in top London music stores. If he hadn't, I probably wouldn't have seen it!*

First of all, at 8.5 lbs. in weight, Dave Hill's guitar is quite heavy by most modern standards - courtesy of an impressive piece of rusty-coloured maple tone-wood for the body. Two pickups - a humbucker in the bridge position and a single-coil variant in the neck - are surrounded by a large, white scratch-plate. Two volume and two tone controls framed by another white plate complete the look.

The correct choice of tone-wood is another skill that a guitar maker must learn and apply. While many components undoubtedly combine to create the tone of an electric guitar - the pickups, the bridge and strings etc - the basis for everything is invested in the wood from which the body, neck, fingerboard and headstock are made.

While electrical components and hardware can be experimented with and changed with time to suit different requirements, the wood from which a guitar is constructed is there from the beginning for that instrument's life.

In addition to the differing sonic and acoustic qualities of the various woods available to a guitar maker, there are other factors that affect the choice: availability, size, tradition and stability being some of the more important.

As a general rule, the favoured electric guitar body tone-woods were always mahogany, maple, alder and swamp ash - certainly in the earliest days of solid body guitar construction. These are all hardwoods. In later years, cheaper instruments have been made using non-hardwoods such as pine or plywood. Even cardboard has been seen in guitar construction.

Each of these traditional hardwoods is associated with different qualities in terms of guitar tone. Mahogany is a heavy wood that produces dark, warm, bass-heavy tones. Maple is similarly heavy in weight but, conversely, tends to produce much brighter tones. Alder and swamp ash sit somewhere in the middle and give similar well-rounded tones.

A guitar maker like Sam Li would have sourced an appropriate piece of wood, having carefully studied the integrity for construction purposes and the grain from an aesthetic standpoint, with a view to creating a guitar body.

Guitar makers tend to favour quarter-sawn wood. This is a type of cut made by a saw when large log pieces are being cut into lumber. The log is first cut into quarters lengthwise, leaving four wedges with right angles that meet at more or less the centre of the log.

From each piece, boards are then sawn and these boards - although often expensive - have always been the preferred cuts for guitar makers, not just because of their stability but also because the sawing method often results in straight grains that are appealing visually. From a quarter-sawn board, a guitar body can then be fashioned.

Guitar neck construction has other requirements. Given that it's the neck that's transmitting string tension from the bridge to the headstock, it must be as stable as possible. This is especially true with Fender necks, which have historically been bolted on, unlike early Gibson necks which were set-in via a joint that connected it to the guitar body.

Of all the woods available, maple (and, to a lesser extent, mahogany) has historically been the wood of choice for the necks of electric guitars. Not only does maple facilitate bright tones but it is also dense, hard and strong with uniform grain - all vital qualities in guitar neck construction. Guitar makers would similarly source neck/headstock wood from quarter-sawn boards.

Rosewood has historically been the purist's choice of wood for guitar fingerboards that are inlaid within the neck. Although heavy, because rosewood is also a naturally oily wood, it is often said that the wood's oily pores somehow absorb stray overtones. In addition, rosewood is very smooth and comfortable to the touch.

Sam Li would have had to consider all of the above when selecting materials for his custom guitars. And from what's known about the instruments he made (the majority were maple or mahogany), there was an obvious willingness on his behalf to source the highest quality wood to work with.

Steve Clarke: *Dave Hill's guitar is just beautifully made. The woodwork and finish is second to none. Part of its appeal, I think, is that it's a bit of a Frankenstein. It has elements that echo several styles of guitar which - in combination - work so well together to create something incredible.*

Dave Hill: *I remember his workshop in Soho round by the Chinese restaurants. At one time or another he had to do a little work on the headstock nut which he replaced - that's how I first met him. When I walked in, he said to me 'There's a guitar I haven't seen in a while; I remember making it'. I said 'Yes, and it's a great guitar to play and looks so good too, Sam!' People knew him and his work long before I did.*

Steve Clarke: *Having grown up listening to bands like Sweet, Slade and T Rex, I was always keen to get hold of some of these iconic guitars to see what's inside them. Dave Hill was very generous - for years he had refused to let anybody look at that guitar.*

I was able to tell him a few things about it too – for instance that one of the pickups on it is a Gibson patent from the late '60s and not, as was commonly thought, a PAF pickup. And the pickup in the neck, that everyone on guitar forums always thought was a Strat pickup, actually turned out to be from a

113

Fender Jaguar. Even Dave didn't know that. He said, 'I just thought it was a Strat pickup...but different!'

These artists clearly identified a certain appeal that came with playing and endorsing a custom instrument, hand-made by a true craftsman. Presumably, this made them stand out from the crowd who played the common, factory-built guitars of the time. As such, as early as this was in his guitar-making career, Sam Li's work already clearly came with a serious degree of credibility.

Andy Powell: *I was on the road all the time by '73, and we would swing through these little towns in the Midwest or Texas or whatever, and in those days you could easily pick up instruments in pawn shops. You could get some incredible guitars. I bought a '54 Fender Stratocaster, which was the first production year, for $300. Nowadays it would be worth a few hundred thousand pounds - maybe a whole lot more.*

But my guitar of choice was always the Gibson Flying V. I loved them and I always had a number of them. I had first seen a couple of them in Orange music shop in Denmark Street in 1972. These were brand new '67 models that had been shipped over from the States and were still in the packing cases. As soon as I picked one up, as well as looking bizarre, it sounded amazing. I don't know if it was because there was so much wood in the body or the wings or what it was, but it sounded so incredibly resonant.

But when I started playing them, I soon realised that their problem was always that the headstocks were very fragile because of how they were angled. There was so much tension in the strings that I'd frequently break the headstocks off.

Often overlooked is the relationship between guitar

maker/repairer and the artist. With time and familiarity, there comes an understanding of how an individual likes an instrument to be set up. No two guitarists have their guitar set alike in terms of strings, action, truss rod tension or intonation.

A guitar is, after all, an extension of a person. We know that the connection is partly intuitive, therefore the finer details of its setup is of critical importance. The best setup guys, therefore, are the ones who can quickly assess the needs of the player and then incorporate those wishes into the instrument they're building. Better still, the best setup specialists can also play.

Andy Powell: *Because I made my own guitars, I'd become familiar with repair people and the best ones knew how you like your guitar set up. That skill was intrinsic and Sam, a very skilled player, had it. With time, I eventually plucked up the courage to ask him if he'd consider making me a guitar from scratch. With his booming voice and stern expression, it took me a while to do it. Because he knew what I liked by way of set up, I was confident that he'd be able to lay his hands on a piece of wood and build me something.*

As it turned out, he agreed but with conditions - the main one being that he made no guarantee whatsoever regarding how long it would take. I was fine with that.

Powell not only wanted something that was playable and custom-built but he also craved an item that would stand out from a performance perspective. Wishbone Ash were playing arenas after all; this Sam Li guitar would be seen, admired, on a nightly basis by many thousands. As such, it had to add panache to a standing, energetic performing artist. Given its unique shape, the Flying V wasn't a guitar one could play very easily while sitting down anyway.

With a body made of limba (trademarked as 'Korina') - a wood lighter in colour than traditional mahogany - the Flying V was a variant of electric guitar first issued by Gibson in 1958. The idea behind it and its sister guitar, the Explorer, was to offer players a more radical, futuristic design of instrument while still, of course, retaining everything that was expected of the brand in terms of build quality and playability.

Initially, while players like bluesman Albert King endorsed the model immediately, the V variant wasn't at all popular and didn't sell well. As a result, it was discontinued the following year. It wouldn't be until the mid-1960s – when guitarists like Dave Davies of the Kinks were looking for an aggressive sound - that the Flying V would be reissued with some modifications designed to cut down on weight. Thereafter, prominent players took to the V shape - Jimi Hendrix and Keith Richards included, at Isle of Wight 1970 and Hyde Park 1969 respectively.

Ken K.K Downing (Judas Priest): *I started playing a V for one reason and one reason only: the look. It looked like the future. And in the context of heavy metal, it was the future. The first one I had was a 1967 – which was one of the Korina mahogany bodied ones. They only made 175 of them between '66 and '69. It was fabulous. Then I had a '70 model. I loved how they played and I still love how they look.*

Nowadays, the first 1958-59 Korina-bodied Flying Vs are some of the most valuable electric guitars on the collector market. Most people have never even seen one far less played one.

Dave Davies (The Kinks): *I knew of Sam Li; everyone did. But I never met him in person!*

Andy Powell: *It did take a long time. It might have been two years in total. I can remember going up the stairs to the workshop on odd occasions when I was back from a tour, just to check in on the progress and get an update. From memory, I think Sam got the basics - the neck and the body - done really quickly. But I think it was the finer, final assembly and finishing that really took the time.*

There's a Guianese proverb that says Nah one time a fire mek peas boil - that broadly means: some good things take a long time to complete. Given that, and Sam Li's reputed attention to detail, it is no surprise that Powell's guitar took a couple of years to finish. Also, given the level of work that was probably on his books at the time, it's highly likely that jobs would have been prioritised according to the nature of the demand.

A 'bedroom guitarist' - as they were often referred to in the trade - on whom there was no pressing time constraint might have to wait longest for a repair. A session player with a backup guitar would perhaps expect to wait a little less long. A rock star with an imminently starting tour would certainly still be at the front of the queue.

However a slow-burn, one-off custom job for a rock star like Andy Powell was at that time - who undoubtedly had a number of alternative instruments to play - would simply have to be fitted around everything else. There were, after all, only so many hours in each day. Either way and whoever the client was, nothing left 19 Gerrard Street unless Sam Li was totally satisfied.

David (Sam's nephew): *I used to go in there and watch him work and I'd often look at something and say 'That looks good.' 'No it's not, it doesn't look right,' he'd say. 'It looks right to me,' I'd tell him. But he wouldn't listen. If the smallest thing was out* *of line, do you know what he'd do? He'd break the whole thing down and start all over again! He was an absolute perfectionist.*

Andy Powell: *When I got it, it was fabulous. It was finished in a kind of tobacco-brown sunburst, which I'd requested. Unlike a standard Gibson Flying V, I'd requested that, instead of having all the hardware mounted on a scratch plate at the front, mine should be rear mounted so that the guitar body was mostly wood. I wanted it to have the appearance of a crafted instrument as opposed to a mass-produced guitar. In a nutshell, I wanted it to echo the luthier. I got the guitar I wanted and I used it.*

Sam then gave me the contact details of a case maker – she made custom cases for violins somewhere in Soho. She had skills that originated from the 19ᵗʰ century, I'm told. They were these beautiful plywood cases covered with leatherette and were specifically made to protect stringed instruments. One was made that followed the exact contours of the guitar. It did look strange – but a rectangular case would have been far too heavy. I remember going through an airport in Louisiana some months later and this big, black security officer looked at me and said 'Hey boy, what is that? You got a giant snake catcher there?' It was admittedly an odd shape.

Another bespoke Sam Li custom guitar was out there on the stages of the world in the hands of someone who genuinely appreciated the man's skills with wood. It says a lot that a musician should choose a handmade instrument over a trendy, big brand name too. Given its origin, the relationship continued beyond the initial sale.

Andy Powell: *I often saw Sam thereafter but really, because the guitar was so well built, it didn't need much in the* *way of maintenance. I did have him add a few enhancements later, however. While I was out on tour in America, I went to the Gibson factory and managed to acquire a few parts that I wanted customised. I remember taking them back to Sam and seem to recall that he managed to have them gold-plated.*

Looking back on my time with Sam, I now think that what appealed to me most was his manner. Some people in the business can be sycophantic, all over you. He was the opposite. It was like going to see the schoolteacher. He just cut through any of the artifice and I'm sure that shocked some people at first. I liked it though because I knew there was no BS there. And, believe me, there was enough BS around the music business at that time!

While Sam Li's relationship with Francis Rossi of Status Quo had continued from a repair and setup perspective, unlike other musicians who crossed Sam's threshold, Rossi apparently never broached the subject of having a guitar custom made by Sam.

Francis Rossi: *I don't think I got that far with him. Instead I lost contact with him along the way and that's one of the worst things I could have done. In the latter years I could have really done with his advice. I'm sure he'd have looked at some of my guitars and told me that they're past their sell-by date, because they probably are. I feel like slapping myself for letting him go but that's what happens in life.*

Gordon Hawtin: *I remember Sam asking me to come into his place whereupon he told me that he had a guitar for me. He said that he'd made it for Eric Clapton but apparently Clapton didn't want it. It was a Telecaster body in a really nice speckled*

119

blue colour with a maple Fender Jaguar neck - which was very rare at the time - with pearl inlays. It had a Strat pickup and a Telecaster back pickup. He wanted a hundred quid for it and, in truth, in those day guitars weren't worth very much. For example, I bought a '63 Stratocaster for a hundred quid but had to give it back because I couldn't afford the HP payments! Nowadays it would be worth a few grand. I bought the guitar from Sam all the same.

Anyway, that same day I discovered that Sam had also made two Sam Li custom Telecasters that he offered to Francis Rossi and Rick Parfitt of Status Quo for about a hundred quid each. I know this because I was in his workshop when they came in to pick them up to try them. These were based on a Fender Telecaster, with a handmade body. Then he'd put a Fender Telecaster neck on them and sometime later I even saw one with a Stratocaster neck. The guys in Status Quo took these two guitars away, played them and then took them back to Sam sometime later. Could have been two weeks, could have been a month. One was a green one from memory, but definitely not the same green one Rossi was often seen using.

I have no idea what happened to those guitars but it wouldn't surprise me at all if they got slipped into stock at one of the guitar shops and sold as Fenders. That kind of thing happened in those days! Mine I sold to a guy in a local band who I saw playing Beach Boys' covers. He gave me cash and I bought a Les Paul Junior.

While it was his ability with guitars that first attracted new clients and interested observers from around the London guitar scene in the late '60s and early '70s, it appears that the quirkiness of Sam Li's personality was a source of a certain amount of fascination also. There were, after all, probably few like him - with that offbeat combination of dapper attire and outwardly serious demeanour, with quick wit and a wicked sense of dry humour.

Equally, given that Sam was one level above the street and involved in painstaking, solitary work from day to day, there's a suggestion that there was a reciprocal element to these relationships that appealed to him. Diversity in any job is key. And with the range of people of all ages walking up those Soho stairs in these days, there was surely no shortage of that.

Tommy Willis (former tea boy at Sound City, guitarist in Q Tips, Chris Rea's guitar tech): *I was sixteen or seventeen at the time and a bit wild. I was working as the tea boy in Sound City. To get out of the shop, I used to get sent round with all the repairs and stuff to give them to Sam. So when they used to send me out for that, I would spend a good hour or two in his workshop killing a bit of time. He was a lovely man and very straightforward. And I got the impression that he actually liked the weirdness of people like me, as serious as he was. I think he even attracted that kind of person.*

Fiona Beattie: *Being a quiet, unassuming man he had presence and got on well with big personalities.*

As he'd done with other clients, Sam Li allowed Tommy Willis into not only his professional life but also into his personal life - albeit on a superficial level.

Tommy Willis: *As time passed we got to know each other better. I think he took pity on me a little. He and I would go to the Curry Centre along the street - that was our favourite place. That's where I first learned about the concept of splitting bills.*

121

Sam Li taught me a few things.

Eventually, given that I was an aspiring guitarist at the time, I started getting him to do a bit of work for me. I knew he was a good jazz player because, in my early days at Sound City, one of the directors - a guy called Brian - was a bit of a jazz player. He had a Gibson 175 that he'd bring in to work. Whenever possible, he'd either go round Sam's or Sam would go into his office. There they'd play a bit of jazz together. He intrigued me.

As a blues player, I was always bending strings. I used to get him to take the middles out of the necks of the guitars so I could bend the strings further. He'd stare at me and say 'Why would you want to? Play it properly!' In general I'm not sure what he thought of rock music. He'd often say 'Loud...too loud.' He hated loud!

Inevitably, we had a few run-ins over the years. One in particular springs to mind. There was a guy called Dougie Ellis who was the manager of Sound City at the time. I believe he had previously worked at Selmer with Sam. I don't remember what the exact circumstances were, but Sam ended up making him a guitar a bit like a Gibson SG. He seemed to put it all together quite easily.

Doug Ellis: *I was working at Sound City by this time. I bought a Gibson neck from somebody who had it removed from his guitar because he didn't like the profile. He had a replacement made for him by Dick Knight. I decided to use this on a solid body guitar and thus bought a lovely block of mahogany, intending to do the building myself. I used to play around with that sort of thing but wasn't that good at it.*

If I remember rightly, I drew around a Gibson SG, overlapped the sides of this bit of mahogany, I might add, then

I started to shape the body into an SG shape. The block was thicker than the SG but not quite wide enough, so the shape was 'clipped wing.' I can't remember how far I got with it. I'm sure I could have continued with it and achieved something; I've made guitars since. But in conversation with Sam, who didn't have a particularly high regard for my skills as a luthier and consequently found all of this to be highly amusing, it was agreed that he'd undertake to do most of the job on my behalf. He certainly did the neck fitting and I'm pretty sure he did some of the body shaping also. He would have certainly done the pickup recesses and, of course, the routing for the control area.

Given that it was to be a set-in neck, common to Gibson, the pitch of it had to be exactly right given that the Tune-o-matic bridges didn't offer too much by way of adjustment, particularly laterally. All in all it was a very sensible move on my part to ask Sam to do the work as it was a valuable Gibson neck and a very nice piece of wood. Sam, of course, made a wonderful job of it. I later sold it (can't remember to whom) because I needed some cash. I wish I still had it.

Tommy Willis: *From that day forward, after seeing Doug's guitar, I pestered him into making me an SG - that is until I saw the Flying V he'd made for the guy in Wishbone Ash. At the time I was young and loved the idea of a flash guitar. Not just that, it was an amazing guitar and you didn't see many around. I was harassing him: 'I've got this piece of wood. Can you make this?' type of thing. And in the end he went away and he did it for me.*

Funnily enough, we fell out because it took ages. I was waiting for two or three months. About half way through this time I had a gig in the Marquee and wanted to use that guitar. I went round there and he said 'No, it's not finished yet, it's not even got any lacquer on it.' I took it anyway and brought it back after a couple of weeks. He went absolutely mad at me. But we always made up in the end. I loved him to pieces.

Both Flying Vs made by Sam Li in the 1970s still exist. The model made for Tommy Willis is a fantastic piece of craftsmanship. With a solid mahogany body in a cherry sunburst colour, the guitar still retains Sam Li's favoured Grover machine heads.

Unlike the standard Gibson-made Vs that came with two humbuckers - one at the neck and one at the bridge - this particular Sam Li custom V has just one Gibson humbucker in the middle position. To this day, the guitar is in first-class condition.

The guitar made for Wishbone Ash's Andy Powell is similar in that it's a 'burst design but different in that it came with the more familiar two-humbucker set-up. Both Vs were fitted with a tremolo arm.

Andy Powell: *I ended up selling it to a guy called Jimmy Martin - he's a songwriter from Luxembourg. H was a massive fan of the band and, when I ended up with this big collection of guitars, I decided to sell some of them in order to build a recording studio at a farm I bought in Buckinghamshire. Anyway, this gentleman, Jimmy Martin, has still got the guitar, I believe.*

Jimmy Martin (musician, producer): *I'd owned Flying Vs since the 1980s. I always just loved the shape of them. Even though it was so long ago that Jimi Hendrix first showed up with one, they still look out of this world. I was also a huge Wishbone Ash fan in the '70s and I'd got to know Andy so, when I was over in England staying with him at his farm in the summer of '86, he showed me the guitar. I loved it straightaway and I bought it from him right there and then.*

I could immediately tell that this guitar was nothing like a stock Gibson guitar. This Sam Li guitar was absolutely beautifully made. The inlays were wonderfully finished - as was the headstock. And it played beautifully also. I don't have big hands so the neck was perfect for me. It was all so smooth.

I ended up selling it and I now wish I hadn't. I was moving; I had lots of guitars and so at first, I put it on ebay. Soon afterwards, Andy got in touch and said that there had been a lot of feedback through the Wishbone Ash site about his guitar being advertised on ebay, so I took it off. Not long afterwards, this German guy offered me cash and I just sold him it. I've since heard that he too has sold it on. That's the last I heard of the guitar. It was in perfect condition when it left me. Again, I really wish I still had it!

* * *

'The looks ah de pudding is not de taste'
(Not everything is as it appears.)

It's clear to see that, while some instruments have simply disappeared, other guitars made by Sam Li are out there in the hands of collectors and players alike. Great effort was made to locate and analyse all of them.   Equally, and rather bizarrely, guitars not made by Sam Li appeared during the process of researching the man's life.

In May of 2019, word got back that a twelve-string acoustic guitar bearing his name had been purchased on Craigslist in Cincinnati, Ohio for a remarkably small sum of money.

On first consideration, the location didn't raise any particular suspicion. His instruments have, no doubt, become distributed worldwide given how long it has been since he made them. The fact that this was an acoustic guitar was surprising however - especially given that no mention had been made of Sam's expertise in this particular field.

There is, of course, evidence of him fixing struts in acoustic instruments and there's no doubt that he would have set many such guitars up. But did he build any from scratch? The suggestion that he might have was certainly an interesting development. Pictures were, therefore, requested for the purposes of provenance.

The images that came back showed an undoubtedly well made, if rather dirty and bedraggled, acoustic guitar with extremely elaborate inlay work on the guitar's back, the headstock and the fret-board. It looked stunning. Painstaking and highly skilled work had clearly gone into this guitar which, at the time, had a structural issue whereby correctly tuning all twelve strings caused some kind of odd structural instability in the guitar's body.

While that problem could probably have been fixed, what was harder to remedy was the fact that, after much build-up, the pictures revealed that the writing on the headstock actually appeared to say Sam Lu rather than Sam Li. Despite this unfortunate news, the new owner still wondered if the guitar in their possession could be a genuine Sam Li!

In all likelihood, this beautiful instrument has no connection whatsoever with Sam Li. While the name on the headstock is uncannily similar, it seems likely that this is simply a bizarre coincidence - albeit a bit of research online found absolutely no record of a guitar manufacturer by the name of Sam Lu or indeed any other guitars bearing that same inscription.

It'll remain an unsolved mystery...

CHAPTER TEN

With retrospect, 1967 until early '73 represented Sam Li's career sweet spot. His timing was perfect in the sense that few could do what he did; he could hardly have been better placed in the heart of Soho. As such, the business of rock music was good to him and he reciprocated in kind. Through his own skills and shrewd use of contacts, he'd carved out a very lucrative niche for himself.

Jude Dawson (former musician, employee in London guitar shops and now a vet): *I was just a young guy, trying to make something happen as a bass player in London. My mate Chris got a job in a little shop called Modern Sound - part of the Arbiter group - just on the edge of Denmark Street. He would tell me about all the exciting day-to-day happenings in the shop. I was really envious. One day he called and asked me if I wanted a job as tea boy. This would have been in January 1974.*

It was here that I first met Sam Li, although obviously I'd heard of him because when I was playing in my band and my bass needed an adjustment, my mate Chris said 'Just take it to Sam Li.' 'Who's Sam Li?' I asked. 'He's really cool and he's a wizard with guitars.' I went in there and I'll never forget that he picked up a screw, dipped it in some tallow and turned to me and said 'This will slide in like greased-lightning, mate.' Mate was a word I always used. I think he used it to me as a jokey term of endearment. He always called me mate thereafter – in that deep voice of his!

Fiona Beattie: *Sam was always a stickler for speaking correctly. He would always pick us up on slang or poor enunciation. Sam had an interest in words, enjoyed crosswords and regularly played Scrabble with members of the family who were all very competitive.*

Jude Dawson: *Sam used to come in and out of the shop over a period of a few months. We actually became mates. The beauty of it was we could go out to a bar - and there was a place in Macclesfield Street called De Hems that we liked - and we'd just sit and talk about life despite the fact that I was maybe twenty and he was perhaps forty-five.*

What was so unusual about this friendship was that everyone I knew was part of a group of people. Sam was part of no group. We'd just sit, chat and put the world to rights. I remember one conversation where I referred to the fact that his sister was a Salvationalist. Sam's mouth dropped. 'How did you know that?' he asked me. 'You told me last night!' I replied. Sam smiled, with emotion in his eyes. 'So few people listen,' he said.

In late 1973 or early 1974, however, something changed. While business was undoubtedly plentiful and his reputation was certainly glowing, unknown circumstances dictated that Sam Li had to, or chose to, leave his premises on Gerrard Street. Whether there were issues with the lease/landlord or there was something structurally amiss with the workspace itself, nobody knows.

And then there's another possibility altogether. Was Sam Li becoming jaded with the frenetic life he was living? These questions, obviously, will remain open to a degree of conjecture.

There's even some doubt as to where Sam actually went after he left Gerrard Street. It was circulated that he had relocated to a temporary workshop in Great Portland Street around this time. However, nobody recalls going there - not even family - to the extent that one wonders whether Sam Li was ever there at all. No postcards or letters sent to that address have ever been found; no photographs of where he worked remain. Sam Li might as well have disappeared.

Pete Cornish: *I sadly lost touch with Sam when he left Gerrard Street. Nobody really knew why or when he left. Inevitably, there were various rumours flying around Shaftesbury Avenue at the time. And one of them was that Sam had sold all his tools, bought a Gibson L-5 and gone off on a cruise ship somewhere playing Bossa Novas!*

The idea of Sam Li taking off and playing Bossa Novas out on the high seas sounds like an urban myth. Or fake news, even. Either way, Sam Li soon resurfaced...

Via information written on postcards that have been found since Sam Li's passing in 2005, we know for certain that, from a business standpoint, he definitely wasn't operating out of a Great Portland Street premises by August of 1974. Instead, having relocated the family home to Harrow, his given work address was 36 Rosslyn Hill, Hampstead, NW3 - certainly by the 11th August. Today, the room Sam operated from is a dental surgery.

Tommy Willis: *I lost contact with him soon after he moved. I was probably in my twenties when I became a pro musician. I wanted to make albums and things. Life goes so fast. And at the time you just take everything for granted. I mean, the people I met in those days were unbelievable. Sam was one of them.*

The reason for this unusual move to workshop premises so

far away from where he'd been doing successful business in Soho was initially unclear. However, after considerable investigation, it became apparent an existing professional relationship was at least part of the reason for his decamping to the suburbs.

Certainly there was an obvious risk attached to relocating so far from the heart of the music scene in Soho. As affluent a suburb as Hampstead was, it was far from being the day-to-day stomping ground of the musicians of the time. However, Sam Li was shrewd. Perhaps there was some kind of added security with the move that was acting as an incentive he couldn't ignore?

Phil Harris: *I honestly think that Sam had had enough. He was fundamentally a quiet guy and very astute. In Soho, it wasn't like people phoned to make an appointment. He'd have people knocking on his door day and night - 'I'm doing a gig tomorrow night, can you do this, can you do that...' After a few years, I think it started to piss him off.*

The progressive rock band Yes were formed in 1968 by singer Jon Anderson, bass player Chris Squire, guitarist Peter Banks, keyboard player Peter Kaye and drummer Bill Bruford. This initial incarnation of the band primarily performed re-workings of pop, blues and jazz songs along with a few original recordings of their own.

Having signed with the Atlantic label in early 1969, Yes released their debut eponymous album later that year. It included original compositions alongside cover versions of 'Every Little Thing' by The Beatles and 'I See You' by the Byrds.

In 1970, guitarist Steve Howe joined the band. Born in Holloway, North London in 1947, having absorbed his parents' eclectic record collection that included Bob Dylan, Les Paul, Chet Atkins and Barney Kessel, Howe acquired his first acoustic guitar from a shop in Kings Cross at the age of twelve.

Having had nothing in the way of formal teaching, Steve Howe arrived on the London scene at the age of seventeen as a member of a blues band called The Syndicats, who were managed by Joe Meek. By this time, he had already acquired, among others, a 1964 Gibson ES-175D – the hollow body arch-top guitar with which he is now synonymous. Howe's band later changed its name to Tomorrow whereupon they also switched styles to more of a progressive, psychedelic sound in keeping with those times, before finally splitting in 1967.

Howe then auditioned for Yes in 1970, following the departure of his predecessor, Pete Banks. Thereafter, Steve Howe enjoyed three lengthy stints in Yes across the decades, having left at various times to embark on other ventures with 'Supergroups' such as Asia, GTR and Anderson, Bruford, Wakeman and Howe.

Steve Howe: *I think that Sam and I first met in Selmer in around 1968. In those days there was a circle of people who hung out and worked in guitar shops and so the best place to be was in one of these shops because then you could both meet people and try out guitars. When Sam left, I remember that, when things went wrong with a guitar, they'd send us to his workshop. I'd have probably just joined Yes at that time. There are two things I remember pretty clearly. The first is that there was an overwhelming smell of glue and the other was that he was absolutely fanatical about Grover machine heads.*

Located on the headstock of a guitar, machine heads, also called tuners - in simple terms these are geared pieces of apparatus for tuning a stringed instrument using string tension - with one corresponding to each of the six strings.

It was as far back as the late 1800s that Albert Deane

Grover started inventing and patenting tuning accessories for mandolins, dulcimers and banjos.

In 1922, as guitar manufacturing took off, A.D Grover became one of the leading innovators in machine heads, continually refining the designs to ultimately create a tuner sealed in a metal shell. In 1952, A.D Grover became Grover Musical Products. They are, to this day, one of the market leaders in guitar tuners.

Steve Howe: *The gearing on them was good, and they allowed you to have accurate tuning, but they were big and needed slightly bigger holes created in the headstock. Anyway, Sam did it and did various other repairs. I trusted his judgement.*

In the months after Sam left his Gerrard Street workshop and then apparently having spent time in Great Portland Street premises, there must have been a conversation between him and Steve Howe.

Whether the initial idea was simply about new premises or whether there was a broader plan whereby Sam would become the go-to repairer/maintainer for Howe's reputedly massive guitar collection is unknown. However, one way or another, it wouldn't be long before Sam Li was installed in one or possibly two of Steve Howe's properties in the Hampstead area.

Gordon Hawtin: *The next thing I heard about Sam was that Steve Howe had opened up some kind of antique instrument shop in Pond Street and he'd seemingly set Sam up in there to do guitar repairs. It was a huge building with what used to be a nightclub underneath. I knew this because I lived at 32 Warwick Mansions - on the corner of Pond Street and Southend Road.*

At that time I was trying to become a bit of a singer/

songwriter, and I was writing what I thought were some pretty amazing songs, and the reason I thought I was doing that was because there was a plaque near my front door that said George Orwell had lived there. I thought I was getting some of Orwell's creative mojo - but it turns out he lived downstairs and worked in a bookshop. And the real reason I was writing good songs was because I couldn't get a bloody TV picture half the time. The Royal Free Hospital was blocking my aerial!

Anyway, for whatever reason, it didn't work in that Pond Street building. Sam was only there a short time before the next thing I knew was that he'd been set up in another place on Rosslyn Hill. It was on the top floor above a toyshop. I don't know all the details, but it always seemed to me as if Steve Howe set him up with no rent to pay - with some kind of agreement where he'd take a percentage of Sam's business. That's the way it appeared.

Steve Howe: *Something happened whereby he must have said something like 'I need to get out of here.' I had a property and I couldn't do what I wanted with it. I wanted to have a guitar sales shop above another shop in Hampstead. But the council told me that the first floor could only be used for retail and that it had to be something like a dentist or, as it turned out, a guitar repair workshop. So, from memory, I set Sam up there with some kind of arrangement that I don't remember. He might have been paying rent - as he wasn't directly working for me.*

Roger James: *There was a big warehouse that I believe belonged to Yes. All I remember is that it might have been somewhere in Bayswater. I used to go there. Sam's office was upstairs; downstairs was somewhere the band used for all their equipment. They were just becoming massive. So they had this space and it had all these Harley Davidsons for the outriders and* *the trucks, etc. in it. They even had all the scenery and all the lighting kept there and, from Sam's office, you could see down in to the warehouse. From the mid '70s or early '70s, I think.*

Peter Finbow: *After he moved out of Gerrard Street, I have a vague memory of helping him move equipment into a temporary place in Talbot Road, Bayswater.*

Whether there's some confusion and the Yes warehouse as described was the same property that Sam Li was said to first occupy after he left Gerrard Street is unclear.

What is certain is that, from 1974, Sam was installed in the first floor property above a health food store on Rosslyn Hill.

From there, as he'd done in Gerrard Street, he'd repair and perhaps make more of his own custom guitars for clients on request. Whether some of his existing Gerrard Street clients, other than Howe himself, followed him is an unknown. As the crow flies, it's a 3.7-mile journey, quite a trek on foot from Central London - albeit easily accessible on the Edgware branch of the London Underground Northern line. Suffice to say, musicians and guitar types found him nevertheless. Word soon got out.

Richard Thompson was one of them. Now considered to be one of music's greatest ever guitar players - a guitarist's guitarist if there ever was one - Thompson was born in Notting Hill Gate, West London in 1949.

Richard Thompson (Fairport Convention, all round guitar legend): *As far as setup goes, the first and foremost thing I want is evenness. The strings should be evenly spaced, each fret the same height, the distance from the string to the fret should be consistent, the strings should be a consistent height across the fingerboard or follow the curvature evenly. Then I want strings* *the same height at the bridge. The action, i.e. the distance from the strings to the frets, should be comfortable, not too high, not too low, and is what the player is used to. As a rule for me, I want low for acoustic and high for electric, so I can bend notes. I want no buzzes. I want the neck to feel smooth front and back.*

When I was living in Hampstead, Sam was just across the road in Steve Howe's place. I needed a re-fret done on my '59 Strat - from memory I used it on the Hokey Pokey album and perhaps a few subsequent recordings. It was Jerry Donahue who suggested I use Sam and so I went in, dropped it off and picked it up when it was ready. There was no conversation. But it was a very good re-fret - and I remember noticing that the fret-board was more highly polished than I was used to, before or since.

Phil Taylor (Dave Gilmour of Pink Floyd's guitar tech): *We used Sam to do some repairs and set the action on some of David's guitars in the mid-'70s. He was a nice man. David liked the way in which Sam set the action up and, when I spoke to him about this when he had just set up David's Workmate Esquire, I asked him exactly how he did the setups. Sam just looked at me a little bemused and told me that it was simple: he just set the guitar up so that it felt good to play.*

Like many guitarists, Gilmour amassed an interesting collection of guitars across his career. One report suggested that this collection numbered in excess of 130, some of which, the aforementioned Workmate Esquire included, Sam Li would have worked on at some point in the 1970s.

In June of 2019, 126 of those guitars went to auction in New York, with all proceeds being donated to Gilmour's own charitable trust, ClientEarth, which tackles global issues such as climate change, famine and homelessness. The total raised was in excess of seventeen million pounds - with a record fee in excess of three million pounds paid for a 1969 black Fender Stratocaster.

David Gilmour (Pink Floyd): *Nice chap, he was above Steve Howe's health food shop on Haverstock Hill. He had this ability to get them to feel good!*

Like Gilmour, Steve Howe admits to have started collecting guitars - in his case as far back as 1964. He has since produced a detailed guitar-related book that documents not only every guitar model, its place of purchase and specification at purchase but also any technical or other changes made to each guitar during his tenure.

Given Steve Howe's reputed propensity for tinkering with his guitars, his guitar book is an absolute mine of detailed information. Not just that, Howe, as great a musician as he was, by his own admission just didn't have the required technical know-how to do much more than basic guitar maintenance.

Francis Rossi: *I've heard that Steve Howe is very sacred about his guitars. I always thought he must have sponsored Sam somewhat and thought 'I need this guy' - because I believe he had a shitload of guitars. I remember reading somewhere he wanted to be buried with his guitar. I'm not quite that much in love with mine!*

It is entirely possible, therefore, that Howe saw potential for a situation whereby two needs could be fulfilled. Sam could continue his freelance business out of premises owned by Howe. Then, at the same time, given that Yes was likely to be on the road for the majority of the mid to late '70s, Sam could also maintain and modify, if required, guitars that were in Howe's ever-growing collection.

On this basis, this offer of a partnership of sorts, if made, would have been a no-lose position for Steve Howe in that he'd have someone he could rely on, in his premises, looking after his guitars.

Equally, it might have been attractive to Sam Li at that time too, as we know that he and his wife Babs had two children of their own by 1974. While there were, no doubt, aspects of the bustle of Soho that Sam would miss, perhaps a more sedate and structured situation in the relative peace and quiet of one of London's most affluent city suburbs appealed more given his position in life?

Steve Howe: *I respect guitar repairers because I had found out from experience that, if I tried to do something myself, I'd bodge it. I was notorious for bodging guitars and a few of them turned out rubbish because of that. So I decided not to do it and let someone else do the repairs.*

Again, everything had to have Grover machine heads - including a Gibson L4C electric mandolin. Really that was just a bizarre idea because it was a tiny thing and, as I said, Grovers are big heads. Then he put them on a Gibson Super 400 and a Gibson ES33512. He had connections. You weren't dealing with somebody who was continually going to ask you where to get things. If you said to him 'I want to do this,' he would source everything. He'd either have it or source it, or at least know where to get it.

As the mid '70s rolled on, with Yes in their richest vein of creativity and success on the back of commercially successful albums like Tales from Topographic Oceans, Relayer and Going for the One, it appeared that Steve Howe was comfortable enough with Sam Li's work to give him pretty much free rein to modify, repair or enhance any of the guitars in his vast collection of rare and expensive guitars.

Steve Howe: *We did several what I'd call 'projects'. One of them was on an extremely rare guitar called a Gibson FDH. Very rarely do you see these. (Note: the FDH is an archtop guitar made by Gibson in the 1930s for music publishers Francis Day and Hunter). For some reason I wanted a pickup so Sam had to put this enormous Charlie Christian pickup in the guitar. We thought it was great but eventually I gave it back to Gibson to renovate. They didn't do a great job of it.*

And there's the Les Paul that I got Sam to put four pickups on. It was the only Les Paul with four pickups in the world and my thinking behind it was that I could create quadrophonic sound - with each pickup sending sound to its own speaker. I got them from Gibson and got Sam to fit them and then, later, I restored it back to its original state and sold it.

The other crazy one was the Vox bass. I liked playing bass and have played it on a few of my own records. Anyway, we had this short scale Vox bass and I got fed up with it to the point where I asked Sam to put three pickups on it. We left the original Vox pickup on then added, from memory, a Rickenbacker pickup and one other six-string guitar pickup of some kind. Basically it ended up as this non-conformist chunk of wood that we essentially ruined.

Francis Rossi: *It's funny because I remember Steve Howe coming to see us at Wembley. They used to try and bring other celebs in to raise profile in the old days. I remember him coming up to me and you could see that he felt really bloody awkward. He must have thought 'What a sack of shit this lot are.' And he*

*said to me, 'Oh, you're really quite fast, aren't you?' 'You really
don't have to say stuff like that,' I replied. So he must have been
thinking what he could possibly say to a bloke who can't play a
guitar particularly well compared to what he could. 'Ah, thanks,
alright,' he said. And that's the first and last time I ever met Steve
Howe.*

Confronted with Steve Howe's at times somewhat off-
the-wall ideas for guitar modification, Sam Li mostly seemed
to be happy in his role as a willing accomplice. Sam, after all,
understood guitars and wasn't afraid to push the boundaries of
what could be done with them from all perspectives - electronics
and hardware specifically. But even he had his limits.

Steve Howe: *I used to go in there and say 'I want to do
this.' And then I'd basically look for the level of shock in his face.
But from that perspective, Sam was very resilient. If it couldn't
be done, he'd say so. Anything else we'd sit and discuss how we
were going to do the wiring and from where we intended to
source these parts. In general we always just pinched things from
Gibson. Consequently, over time I started collecting guitar parts:
I had drawers full of bridges and machine heads, etc. Sam was
very, very good at that kind of work.*

Roger James: *I didn't see him for a while, and someone
said he's moved to Hampstead, on Hampstead Hill (Note: it was
Rosslyn Hill), and I remember going up the hill from Camden to
a place. It was on the right hand side. It was up some stairs and
he had all his tools there.*

*From then on, Sam always fixed my guitar. He was
a craftsman. I used to say that everybody from Hank Marvin
downwards (because he was my idol) used to use Sam Li. He was*

the business.

One day I went to him and I said 'Look, I've got this Stratocaster...' If you know Stratocasters, they fit your body, the contour, it's like a woman; it's so beautifully curved. I also had this quite rare, imported Telecaster - a 1963 or '64 model, and if you know Telecasters, they're a bit like a plank with a cutaway here and a cutaway there.

So I said to him 'Can you make this like my Stratocaster?' Part of me expected him to say 'OK, yes alright, leave it with me.' But instead he talked me out of it completely. 'No, I wouldn't do that. I really wouldn't do that,' he said. On reflection, I'm really glad he did because I would have ruined it. At the time I just said, 'OK, Sam.' You respected him because he was The Man and, if he said don't do that, you didn't do it. You would never say 'Please, do you mind?' You'd never say that. Once he'd told you, that was it.

Hank Marvin (The Shadows): *I met him a few times in the '70s, and he subsequently set up a guitar or two.*

Edmond Leu: *I remember being in the Hampstead shop one day and these guys from the band Sweet Sensation were there. Although I had no idea who they were at that moment, I was later told that they'd had a big hit around that time called 'Sad Sweet Dreamer.' Anyway, Sam was talking to them and then, when they left, he turned to me with a grin and said: 'They're useless. They can't sing!'*

Phil Harris: *I was playing in a band by this time and I ended up living on Thurlow Hill in a flat with our rhythm guitarist and his girlfriend who happened to be Neville Chamberlain's granddaughter. I heard Sam was working up that way. I used to* *pop in there to look at the guitars and Sam, if I remember rightly, was upstairs. I got the impression he was doing a lot of custom stuff for Steve Howe.*

I was having trouble with throwing guitars at things and all the rest of it. In those days nothing really mattered. You'd do anything to get a reaction. So I remember bashing frets in and in those days you had no money and so you'd sort of say to Sam 'Can you, err, just replace the damaged frets? He always thought that was highly funny because you can't just do that. Other than that there wasn't much joviality about him up there. You wouldn't share a laugh with him. He was the opposite of a Carry On movie. I mean he was pleasant but there was no palliness whatsoever. He was just: 'This is what's wrong with your guitar. This is what it's going to cost.'

Sam's involvement with Yes wasn't limited to Steve Howe either. Chris Squire, the band's bass player, who sadly passed away in 2015, had various amusing dealings with Sam dating back to the very earliest days of the band in the late '60s.

Famous for his Rickenbacker 4001 bass, Squire once told a story about how, when the flower power era hit in the sixties, he decorated his bass with the appropriate flowered decals and paint. When the movement passed, he wanted the finish removed.

He was then directed to Sam's Gerrard Street workshop whereupon the pattern was sanded off, taking some of the wood with it. Squire then painted the bass a futuristic silver colour and then, after a few years, he seemingly grew tired of that too. Having sanded off the silver paint, again along with some of the wood below, Sam gave the guitar back again.

On the third occasion, this time in Sam's Rosslyn Hill workshop, when Squire was given his newly sanded Rickenbacker 4001 back, he was sent out the door with the words 'Please don't do it again' ringing in his ears!

Jude Dawson: *In early '75 I went back up to Leeds to try and open a guitar shop up there with a friend. After a few months, we realised it wasn't going to work so I decided to try my luck down in London again. I had no idea where Sam was but I knew he'd left Gerrard Street.*

I ended up getting an interview for a job at Top Gear on Denmark Street as a drum salesman but I honestly knew nothing about drums. 'You know shit all about drums,' the guy interviewing me said. 'What are you doing here?' 'I know lots about PAs and synthesisers though.' 'Really?' he said. 'When can you start?' I'd had some inside information from someone that they were about to open a synthesiser shop on Shaftesbury Avenue and, after a few days, I started.

After a few weeks, I was crouching on the floor, doing something with an amplifier, when all of a sudden these two hands covered my eyes from behind. I turned round and it was Sam Li. At that moment I realised what a good mate he was. I'd been away, lost touch, come back and was feeling a bit lonely in London, truth be told. Most of the people I'd known in the past seemed to have dispersed. So for him to be there and to hug me was really, really great. I think we went out that evening for a few drinks. We were so comfortable around each other.

CHAPTER ELEVEN

Born in New Jersey in 1951, Seymour W. Duncan is the co-founder of the Seymour Duncan Company - a leading manufacturer of pickups and guitar effect pedals based currently in Santa Barbara, California.

In his youth, Duncan was an aspiring guitarist of some repute in his own right. During his early career playing gigs, Duncan made it his business to learn through experience with one incident - where one of the pickups on his Fender Telecaster broke, forcing him to play the rest of the set with only the other - being an event that was particularly significant and informative in the context of his later life.

In the years that followed, Duncan became fascinated with the dynamics and sound variances associated with different pickups. By liaising directly with players for feedback, he was able to experiment with materials and techniques - all with the quest for perfect guitar tone foremost in his mind.

Apparently, at the suggestion of Les Paul, Duncan moved to where everything was happening in the early 1970s - London - to work in the repair/research and development departments at the Fender Soundhouse, a shop owned by Ivor Arbiter on Tottenham Court Road.

Duncan became the go-to guitar repairer in the Fender Soundhouse and, among his jobs over the next few years, would be working on guitars belonging to some of rock and blues music's most celebrated names: Jeff Back, Jimmy Page, Paul McCartney and many more.

Seymour Duncan: *I was working at the Fender Soundhouse in 1974 /1975. I became aware of Sam and I'd visit him for his assistance with some fret repair jobs. I loved seeing his tools. He was such a talented man and a great craftsman too. He had some really cool tricks and that was valuable to me as I was playing guitar and recording at night, primarily with Chris Harley, and modifying instruments by day for musicians like The Who, Jimmy Page and Jeff Beck.*

During his time in London, Duncan also made a guitar, the Tele-Gib, that not only became synonymous with Jeff Beck but was also used on the Blow by Blow album alongside the Sam Li custom. The Tele-Gib was a hybrid born of a bizarre amalgam of components.

Denny Bridges: *I remember the Tele-Gib well. It was one of a number of guitars that Jeff had at that time. He had a white Strat and he had a Gibson Les Paul also. All of them were used - along with the Sam Li custom.*

Seymour Duncan: *Jeff Beck's "Tele-Gib" hybrid guitar was essentially a modified '59 Fender Telecaster that at one time had a slab rosewood fingerboard. The body had been crudely modified; there was no pick-guard, bridge — or anything else serviceable. I removed the fingerboard, replaced it with a 3/16th of an inch piece of maple into which I cut fret slots by hand. The neck was sprayed with nitrocellulose lacquer that I got from Sam.*

Inevitably, like-minded craftsmen like Duncan and Sam Li would end up gravitating together. The '70s London guitar world was a small one. Everybody seemingly knew everyone else.

Seymour Duncan: *I was there the day Sam opened the shop with Steve Howe. He had all of Steve's guitars displayed around the shop and I remember helping him tune them all. Thereafter, Sam would often visit me at the Soundhouse. We'd eat grilled cheese sandwiches with many of the guests that frequently showed up at the store. He was a great man!*

After his time in London, Duncan returned to settle in Santa Barbara in California in 1977, having accrued all manner of fans and potential customers during his sabbatical at the Fender Soundhouse.

A year later, having met and married his wife, Cathy, together they made the decision to start their own pickup rewinding company. As demand for their services grew, Cathy and Seymour launched their own range of humbucking pickups - initially only for Stratocasters and Telecasters.

Two decades later, the company had expanded to the extent that they produced a comprehensive range of pickups for all guitar types in addition to an extensive selection of other guitar accessories such as effects pedals.

Nowadays, the Seymour Duncan Company is a market leader in guitar products with a staff of over one hundred. All in all, a long way from grilled cheese sandwiches with Sam Li et al in 1975.

* * *

Meanwhile, back in London, Sam Li continued working from the Hampstead shop throughout the mid-1970s. He repaired and set up guitars for clients old and new while, at the same time, embarking on various projects at the behest of his landlord, Steve

Howe.

Steve Howe: *He did a Fender Broadcaster and a Telecaster for me. The latter I became famous for and Sam did it all. We put various Gibson bits on it; we fitted a Gibson pickup. He then put this big Gibson switch on a Fender guitar but he did it in a particularly interesting way that I'd learned from some of the early guys who'd customised Fenders in the past. Once he'd done that Fender, I never changed it any way at all. The Broadcaster was an incredibly rare guitar and very, very valuable. We really went to town on that guitar. We put a new bridge on it and rewired a pickup. We did all of these things - and Sam was the only guy who could come up with solutions in these circumstances. In addition, he had his own esteem and always wanted to do good and interesting work.*

There is an odd story with that Telecaster. Sam wired it, and I don't know whether he did it on purpose or whether he didn't, but basically, when you've got two pickups, you have the potential for them to be out of phase - and that in turn gives you a particularly twangy, almost gnarly sound. He did the Telecaster with the back pickup just like a Telecaster is supposed to be but then he modified the front pickup using a Gibson humbucker. I liked that front pickup sound but then I put them together and it went out of phase. I think I said 'Wow, that's out of this world.' And I think he said, 'Well, do you like it? I can put them in phase and it will sound more ordinary' and, in response, I must have said 'No, leave it.'

And lo and behold, on 'Gates of Delirium' on the Relayer album, there's a battle scene in the middle where's there's an awful amount of crashing and the guitar comes in and goes bang, bang, bang. It kind of steps through all the mayhem and that sound was created by what Sam had earlier done with that guitar.

146

I could have easily said 'No, I don't like it. Put it back in phase' and he would have done so. He'd have just switched a couple of wires.

In the background, sadly, there were some issues brewing that would fundamentally affect Sam Li's life and that of his young family also. As productive as his work life was in the earlier days of his Hampstead workshop, all was not well at home.

Fiona Beattie: *I was aware that Sam was always busy and would come home late in the evenings. Whether he was working or just out socialising with friends from the music business, which he may well have done, he was out a lot. I can imagine that this would have caused friction between them and only added to the marital issues.*

Roger James: *There were a couple of times when I took Sam home in the car from the shop in Hampstead. We got chatting and he told me about how he wasn't getting on with his wife and was having a bit of a hard time. I felt he was becoming a bit depressed. I was always a good listener and he seemed to feel comfortable talking to me.*

Fiona Beattie: *In 1977, they split up. It was traumatic for everyone. My mother took her younger son and daughter and went to Australia. Meanwhile, my older brother and I went to stay with our grandmother. Sam phoned me one day and said he still wanted to see my brother and I on a weekly basis. I didn't understand the sentiment at the time but, when I remembered that as an adult, I realised how important that was for him to say it. It was his way of showing that he still cared about us.*

The precise reason for Sam Li's marriage breakdown isn't clear. Like many marriage fractures, there may not have been any single reason.

However, there's an aspect to some of the tension that was much more to do with the era rather than any particular lack of love between him and Babs.

For some period of time, Babs had seemingly been completely exhausted on a daily basis - to the extent that, on some occasions, she'd find it very hard to get out of bed to go to work. Sam, on the other hand, was a man of rigid routine - and an early riser. He was up and dressed at 5 a.m. each day and the suggestion is that, as time passed, he became frustrated. The saddest part of the story is that it wasn't that Babs was lazy. She was working full-time, with two kids, and had very little time for running the house to Sam's standards.

Fiona Beattie: *I think the problems were partly due to my mother's sleep issues. Sam was up at 5 a.m. every day and liked a spotless house whereas my mother needed a lot of sleep and lacked energy and, what with working full time too, she had no time for housework - certainly not to Sam's standards. He thought oversleeping was laziness and, one day, he did not wake my mother just to see what would happen. She awoke at 11 a.m. and was clearly very late for work.*

Later in my mother's life her sleep condition worsened and she was tested for coeliac disease, which was negative. However, we have since found out that this is a family trait, and it is due to a wheat intolerance, which causes crushing tiredness and fatigue. It's all such a shame that they did not know this at the time as they always cared about each other.

The separation and the subsequent departure of his ex-wife and two young children to Australia must surely have taken its emotional toll on Sam. As much as he was always a loving and attentive family man, he was also someone who was, as was evident via his working practices, very proud. As such, it's hard to imagine that Sam wouldn't have shouldered at least some of the responsibility for the failure of his marriage. In all likelihood, he would have very much taken the breakdown to heart.

Fiona Beattie: *Sam was definitely one of life's worriers. He'd take things very personally. If you ever offended him, he'd retreat. For days at a time he'd be silent, as if awaiting an apology. He gave 100 percent but, if he was ever let down, he would rather distance himself from the person rather than say something negative. Birthdays were always very important to Sam and one year my mother got the date wrong and, instead of 5th January, gave him his cards and presents on 6th January. He didn't speak to her for a week after that.*

As if emotional turmoil wasn't enough to contend with, as the '70s transitioned into the 1980s and the music industry moved from Punk into New Wave and beyond, Sam Li's working career gradually started to lose momentum too.

It's hard to assess his emotional state during these early '80s years. The separation had surely left him raw. Sam would have ruminated long and hard as to his role in the breakdown. Not just that, when Babs and the children returned to London from Australia in 1982, the situation was seemingly no less strained - despite the fact that, while in Australia and perhaps missing Sam as the children certainly were, she wrote a letter to her own mother saying that she was considering cancelling the divorce.

Fiona Beattie: *Like most people, my mother had failings. One of them was that she never really did anything to resolve any simmering issues in the family. Consequently, they continued. In the aftermath of the separation, I never once heard Sam say anything negative about my mother. It just wasn't his style to do so. My mother did the exact opposite in terms of painting a distorted picture of Sam to his children.*

In addition to his complex personal life, the wider music world was shifting under Sam Li's feet in a way that meant that craftsmen of his kind were in increasingly less demand as the eighties rolled on.

If any decade was synonymous with big money, it was the 1980s. Bands sold albums by the millions and touring budgets skyrocketed to support elaborate stage shows that the fans turned out in droves to see. Everyone was a winner it seemed - everyone except independent specialists like Sam Li.

The problem was that with bigger budgets came more dedicated tour-related staff. The role of the traditional roadie - the guys loading the gear in and out of venues and handing instruments to their respective bosses from side-stage – was, therefore, evolving quickly. While some no doubt had the ability to change strings quickly and do running repairs, the 80s heaped a hitherto unheard of level of expectation onto the shoulders of these roadies. Pretty soon they were no longer just roadies. Instead, they acquired a new title: guitar technicians.

While some might consider this new title to be just that - a fancy title that meant little - there was a reality to the position that would have a profound effect on highly skilled professionals, like Sam Li, who were previously relied upon to do work on guitars.

Suddenly, guitar techs were expected to be able to set up. Overnight, they were assumed to be able to adjust truss rods and bridges. They'd certainly be able to tune and intonate; they'd probably have a good working knowledge of electronics to boot. Basically, half of the jobs previously undertaken by someone like Sam Li could be done by a guitar tech. Furthermore, most bands of any size could afford to have a tech looking after every band member.

Tommy Willis: *I became a roadie to feed the family really because, as much as I played and toured as a musician, it was hard to pay the mortgage. Initially I did quite well. The truth was, by the time I started in '84 or '85, they were already calling it 'guitar technician'. I wasn't a roadie, I was a guitar technician. When the bands got enough money to actually have different people to look after different aspects of the band like guitar technician, drum technician and all that sort of thing, guitar techs became a lot more specialised in terms of what they did.*

When I worked for Bonnie Raitt and Chris Rea, for example, I used to do a bit of guitar repairs. I wasn't a luthier, obviously - and I'd take the guitar to someone like Sam if I had to - but I certainly got to know how to do a bit of electrical or fret work. And the more you were able to do as a guitar tech, the better chances you had of more work. Your legacy would go with you: 'I've worked for so and so and so and so'; therefore the next job, people would call you up and say 'I've heard you can do this.' The role changed.

Ron Eve: (guitar tech for Mark Knopfler): *I worked as Mark's guitar tech (in the '80s), but I had experience of meeting with Sam when I worked at Gooseberry Studios at 19 Gerrard St in the mid '70s. To be perfectly honest, my memory of that time is 'a bit hazy.' But I went up to the workshop a couple of times. I don't recall Sam doing work on Mark's guitars during my time but, over time, I acquired enough electrical knowledge to understand how it all worked and I went on to wire not only my own 1961 Gibson SG but also a 1969 reissue Les Paul of Mark's, which we later used on the Brothers In Arms album.*

Steve Phillips (The Notting Hillbillies): *Although I never met him personally, I was aware that Mark Knopfler's second Fender Strat was a Sam Li restoration, this being the maple necked and very red (refinished from Fiesta to a hotter red by Sam) Stratocaster that is featured on the famous Sultans of Swing music video, shot at The Old Grey Whistle Test.*

As if the evolving role of the guitar tech wasn't enough of a threat to people like Sam Li, there was another aspect to the music industry that further weakened the guitar repairer/setup guys' position.

When Sam Li first started working in London at Selmer, the separation between musicians and ordinary members of the public was vague at best. In the '60s and most of the '70s, these musicians were just members of the public. As such, they'd walk into guitar shops - as many did - and they'd buy guitars and have guitars repaired in the same places that anyone else might.

As time passed, this separation widened when popular culture made musicians like The Beatles unfathomably famous. Almost overnight, where George Harrison might once have regularly walked into a shop like Selmer to look at guitars (and he did), no longer was that possible. Musicians were forced to behave differently and to go where the general public did not. The Beatles could hardly walk around central London at all, far less hang out in guitar shops. Obviously, this created an elite level of musician that would in time prove irresistible to the instrument manufacturers.

The next stage was the gradual introduction of sponsorship and endorsement arrangements for musicians of a certain standing whereby, instead of buying a guitar in a shop and having it repaired in a workshop, an artist would be given one or more guitars - all of which could be sent back to the manufacturer at any time for major repair, adjustment or replacement. Anything more minor in the way of 'roadside' maintenance could increasingly be attended to by a guitar tech.

The result? The setup guy/repair specialist was gradually bypassed by their most lucrative demographic: the professional musician.

This then would have been the situation facing Sam Li and pretty much any other similar craftsman in the '80s. Professional musicians needed less by way of specialist repairs because their techs could do most of the work. Musicians needed less by way of custom-made instruments because manufacturers gave them away for 'free.' As early as 1983, therefore, there were changes afoot in the music business that would affect everybody.

CHAPTER TWELVE

Just ten years after leaving a thriving business in Gerrard Street, where it must have felt as if the rock music wave could be ridden forever, Sam Li arrived at a point, at just fifty-five years old, where he stood at another key crossroads. To make matters worse, he'd soon have no commercial premises from which to operate either.

Steve Howe: *I can't remember how long he was at Hampstead; he could have been there a year or so. It could have been longer...*

We only had the property for a few years because we lost money. I think I said to Sam 'It's not doing very well; the shop isn't paying.' Looking back, of course, it was crazy to sell as it would be worth a fortune now but, at the time, it was unworkable. Sam must have had to leave whenever it was that we sold it. He could have had a couple of years in there...

It wouldn't be fair to cast aspersions on anyone's version of events. As they say in Guiana, every rope gat two ends. 1983 was, after all, a long time ago.

However, there does seem to be a degree of vagueness about some aspects of the final throes of Sam Li's time in Hampstead in partnership with Steve Howe that certainly poses some questions as to what the precise circumstances were.

Rumours circulated that Howe had left Sam in the lurch somewhat by leaving to set up home in the US while some financial aspects of their arrangement remained unresolved. Others hinted at the idea that Sam Li's heart and mind, for whatever reason, were no longer fully invested in the business and, consequently, he showed up to open the shop and workshop all too infrequently as time passed.

Given that Howe formed the band Asia around this time and the band quickly garnered huge success, it stands to reason that by moving to America as he did, at very short notice, Howe would have given Sam Li little time to find alternative workshop accommodation from which to continue his own repair work.

Gordon Hawtin: *I still lived in the area until the middle of 1982. Then I fucked off to Greece to become a DJ! Wine, women and song as they say. Anyway, I started noticing that Steve Howe's place was open less and less - not that I ever once saw Steve there in person. It just looked like nothing much was happening in the shop.*

Whatever the facts really were, we're unlikely to find out given that Sam Li only ever discussed it at the time with Babs. But the bottom line was that, to all intents and purposes, with no commercial workshop to operate from for the first time since 1960, Sam Li's career as a guitar maker/repairer had taken a swing in another direction.

As if to punctuate it further, a few years after leaving the Hampstead workshop, Sam Li was admitted to hospital having suffered a heart attack in the early months of 1987. After a week in hospital, he was discharged and sent home to recover.

Fiona Beattie: *It came as a huge shock to everybody and* *was totally out of the blue.*

David (Sam's nephew): *I didn't see him as much as I would have liked but I used to call him up on the phone and we'd talk for hours.*

Typical of the man, the last twenty years of Sam Li's business life were something of a mystery. We know he was having some irritating, physical complaints beyond his heart issue. After years of manipulating wood, using hand tools and, later, power tools, the most important part of Sam Li the craftsman's body - his hands - started sending out distress signals.

Like many who have repetitive work with their hands and wrists over many years, Sam Li was steadily feeling the effects of carpal tunnel syndrome - a condition caused by median nerve compression as it passes through the narrow bone channel at the wrist.

Hands that once gripped tightly may have become less effective. Numbness may well have radiated up his arms. Many sufferers complain of discomfort and tightness in the brachial plexus area of the shoulders where the median nerve also passes through tight channels. Pain may have been a constant. Perhaps Sam's sleep suffered too.

Fiona Beattie: *He was having problems with his hand and, at the time, he didn't know what the cause was. Nowadays they call it carpal tunnel syndrome.*

Hampered by discomfort and an inability to sustain the kind of detailed handiwork he once could, it seems certain Sam Li did increasingly less in the way of repairs and setups in the 1990s. Furthermore, there is no evidence of him having made anything by way of custom guitars at all during these years - despite the fact that he would eventually have surgery to address the nerve compression in his wrist.

While he apparently continued to do the occasional guitar-related job from home, made his own furniture and reputedly persisted with his two main loves of playing his jazz guitar and listening to music - particularly jazz greats like Count Basie, Duke Ellington and Oscar Peterson - not much is known about anything else Sam Li did between the early 1990s and his death in 2005. From a business perspective, things had certainly changed. On a personal level, perhaps they had too.

Fiona Beattie: *He spent his days at home making furniture, cooking, watching films and playing music. He also travelled to visit his sisters, nieces and nephews in Canada, the US and Holland. He would also spend time with his friends and visit Babs and the children. And they would visit him.*

Sam's daughter, Jewel: *Having first come over to live with my dad in London in the mid-'60s, after working overseas in Africa, I actually came to London to live when I was maybe in my mid-twenties. During that period, I got a lot of music leads from Sam - some CDs, records, etc. He also invited me to a couple of parties. I guess these were invites from people he'd known in the business. At one time I was living in Chelsea and he used to come and visit me on Sundays. That's when I really got into Astrud Gilberto music. I actually still enjoy and follow similar music to what he liked: the Brazilian and Cuban sound.*

Reconnecting with his daughter, Jewel, who'd been brought up by her mother in Sam's native Guiana, can only have been a good thing. Incidentally, at no point has it ever been suggested that Sam Li deserted his family *when he left Guiana in*

1959.

Indeed, it was understood that, while he'd obviously be living a different kind of life over in London, the relocation was only a positive since he was divorced from his wife; his siblings had married and moved away and, most significantly, his friends were moving to London at the time also.

Clem (Sam's nephew-in-law): *I've always heard of Uncle Sonny from my wife, Mooi, who is his niece, and I finally had the opportunity to meet him during a vacation in London. It was sometime in the mid-'90s. This visit was particularly special because I was returning to him a guitar that I had used during my time as the leader of The 13ᵗʰ Disciple, a gospel contemporary group in Trinidad. I had borrowed the guitar from my mother-in-law who told me that it was handmade by her brother, who we referred to as Uncle Sonny.   On my arrival to his home, I was pleased to meet a diminutive guy with a moustache who welcomed Mooi and me with a huge embrace. On presenting him the guitar, he was somewhat surprised and examined the instrument carefully before playing a few chords. With a smile, he said 'Yes, I made this one!'*

We settled in for a nice visit and I watched and listened as he and Mooi exchanged family stories.   He displayed quite a sense of humour. One story he told me that is still etched in my mind was about the time he received from his oldest sister, Mary, a gift of Guyanese food that included the famous black pudding.

Now, those of you not from the Caribbean will not understand what black pudding is - so let me explain. This rich specialty dish is in the form of a stuffed runner or sausage and is made from pig's or cow's blood. The stuffing consists of rice and meat seasoned with assorted spices. The blood trapped in the runners turns dark when cooked, hence the name 'black pudding.'

It's a Guyanese delicacy that many heartily enjoy.

Mary knew that her brother enjoyed this dish and Sonny recalled that, when she visited, she brought six feet of black pudding for him because she wanted him to enjoy it for a few days. That day he was in heaven and thoroughly enjoyed the first few slices he'd set aside for the day. After a while he decided to go to bed but, while lying there, he said that images of the black pudding kept dancing in his head. In true Guyanese fashion he said 'Man, I couldn't sleep. The pudding kept calling me, calling me, calling me.'

And so, in the middle of the night, Sonny got out of bed, went to the refrigerator and helped himself to several more pieces. He was now wide awake and decided to watch TV. While sitting in his chair trying to digest what he had eaten, the pudding began to call him again. Before he knew it, Sonny had devoured the entire six feet of black pudding. Mooi and I laughed because we understood exactly what he was saying. When people from the Caribbean migrate to other countries, they are so excited when they can consume a meal from their homeland. Uncle Sonny was a perfect example of that experience. This quiet, gentle, unassuming man with a sincere gift of humour left a lasting impression on me.

Jimi King (Sam Li's cousin's son): *I was about six or seven when my dad first took me to the Gerrard Street workshop. It was a Sunday as I recall. Thereafter, I always wanted a guitar as a child and it wasn't until much later that I taught myself to play. Later on in life, I went to the Bass Institute in Acton where I received lessons from a guy called Robbie Burns. As it turned out, he had a guitar that was made by Sam Li. Ever since then, I've been curious. I discovered that Sam was world famous!*

Rob Burns (bass guitar instructor, now living in Dunedin,

New Zealand): *I remember the student, but I never had or used Sam Li gear -as much as I knew about him! I was always a Wal guy.*

In the absence of any anecdotal evidence to suggest that he made any material attempt to revisit guitar repairs/guitar making on a serious commercial level after his heart attack, it seems likely that, in general, Sam Li's latter years were spent in a state of quiet contemplation that was worlds away from the day-to-day hustle of his first fifteen or so years in the guitar repair business.

Whether this was enough for him, we'll never know. But with a guitar in the house, his beloved jazz music to listen to and the daily horse racing form to study, there's a sense that Sam was content to take life reasonably easy - while still retaining a partiality for some of the finer things in life.

Fiona Beattie: *In the late '80s I had moved to a flat on the other side of London. I'd visit Sam and he'd teach me how to make curry, dahl and various Caribbean dishes. He was not only a tremendous cook but he was also very proud of his heritage.*

One day travelling home after work and with cash in my purse to pay for an impending holiday, my purse was snatched. I had planned to visit Sam that evening but had to ring him to cancel and I explained what had happened. A week later, Sam asked me to visit him. It was nice to see him, as usual, but I was surprised when on leaving he handed me some money. It was precisely equal to the amount that I'd had stolen.

On another occasion, I received a bonus at work and decided to give some of it to Sam as a gift. On my next birthday, I was shocked to receive a diamond and ruby bracelet. He had spent the money on me. That was Sam through and through.

Sam Li always loved his family members. Of that there is little doubt. However there's certainly a sense that, in later life, when his stepdaughter was more mature and perhaps more receptive to Sam's subtle ways, their relationship developed touchingly from one whereby a shy, obedient young girl simply placated her stepfather, to one where two intelligent adults were able to relate on an entirely new level.

Fiona Beattie: *I really got to know the real Sam in those latter years. He was so generous, caring and thoughtful. I even bought him a mobile phone so that he could call me any time from wherever he was. The first thing he said was 'Is my new phone as good as yours?' 'No,' I replied, 'it's better. It's the best phone on the market.'*

Typically, given his love of high quality, Sam liked that news and took great pleasure in learning everything about the device and how to operate it. Thereafter, I asked him to ring me every day to let me know that he was OK, and he seemed most happy with that arrangement.

With his dark hair and youthful, lineless complexion, Sam Li's face in his latter years gave him the appearance of a much younger man. His body, however, was no longer young. In his 70s, Sam Li, once the dashing, dapper, young guitar man of Soho, had health issues that slowed him down and he needed help from those around him. Even he couldn't defy time.

Fiona Beattie: *I'd often pick him up to take him to do his shopping and to take him to hospital appointments. He always liked to stop and look at the audio and video equipment. Even in his later years, because he'd had a portable television all of* *his life, he was always fascinated by the newest developments. I remember he and I standing staring at the first flat-screen televisions. He was enthralled.*

* * *

'Nah mind how pumpkin vine run, he must dry up one day.'
(Every life must come to an end one day.)

When Sam Li died in February of 2005, with his stepdaughter Fiona at his bedside, it would be comforting to think that it was only his physical embodiment that passed on.

After all, we know his work and his legacy remain given that many instruments he worked with are out there in the world, being cherished and being played. And through his craftsmanship and the many instruments he touched and fashioned over the years, it would be logical to assume that his spirit lives on also through them.

Few would dispute that Sam Li existed in an era of popular culture - perhaps the last era of its kind that anyone reading his story will experience at least - where detailed, highly skilled craftsmanship was not only viable as a means of making a living but also valued by those who benefitted from it.

Given the direction in which mankind is travelling - with an increasing focus on items being as disposable as they are consumable - it'll surely take a mammoth shift in people's attitudes to reverse the trend. We can only hope...

Kirk Hammett: *I have so much respect for any guitar and guitars in general. My wife took apart a guitar the other day and she took a picture of these fifty pieces spread out all over the carpet. It really bugged me out - 'Oh, no...really!' It really* *stressed me out to consider that now it's just a bunch of parts.*

Andy Powell: *Looking back nowadays, Sam, and the culture he came from, needs a lot of recognition and admiration. I've often thought that automation has gradually taken away our ability to grapple with an object and fashion it - to be brave enough to mess with things. That certainly has become the case with guitars. I've toured India and other places, and I see how, with a car in India, when you don't have a particular part, people will simply fashion a part from a piece of metal. The point being that they're brave enough to do it. So Sam clearly came from a culture where it wasn't too unusual to fix things.*

Doug Ellis: *Sam Li was the best guitar builder and repairer I've ever met. And I've met an awful lot of them over the years. He was really a very, very important man from that era - so highly regarded by all and sundry.*

Dave Hill: *My guitar was an all-round winner with my manager, Chas Chandler, and he knew because he managed and produced Jimi Hendrix. There are things in life which are unbeatable for me and the Sam Li Gibson-shaped SG style guitar I had is unique, a one-off meant for me and in memory of him, I thank you, Sam Li!*

Sam Li approached the art of guitar repair and instrument creation with a level of care and dedication that not only provided his clients at the time with exactly what they wanted but he also did it with a healthy dose of what seemed like uncanny foresight. Perhaps Sam Li was somehow aware of the significance of the era in which he lived and worked? And because he was, maybe he knew that his work would be valued and revered long after he was gone? While vintage guitar collectors didn't exist while he was making custom guitars, perhaps he suspected that one day they just might?

Again, in his absence, we'll never know exactly what he felt. But we can tell by his workmanship - much of which is as good today as it was when he undertook it back in the '60s - that this was a man who knew that whatever he turned his hand to must be able to stand the test of time.

"If yuh plant plantain yuh can't reap cassava'
(You reap what you sow.)

On every level, the decision to leave Guiana in 1959 paid handsome dividends for Sam Li. Not only did he better his life by fully utilising the skills his elder brother Joe had taught him, but he was also able to stay immersed in the world of his beloved music. In addition, his story flies in the face of those who might be a little cynical about the contribution made by immigrants to post-war Britain.

Recent events have illustrated that the incredible contribution made by the Windrush Generation to British life has, at the very least, been undervalued. Indeed, their treatment in recent years, from a legal and humanitarian perspective, has been nothing short of insulting.

Not only were these people welcomed into Great Britain at a time when their skills and work ethic were desperately needed to rebuild a country weakened by war, but they were also legally entitled to come. They first arrived in 1948 with high hopes of a better life and were willing to work long and hard to secure one.

Yet, instead of being humanely integrated and treated as equals, the Windrush Generation was by and large marginalised and dehumanised. Even today, this feeling of being undervalued persists. In 2019, after a life of nothing but contribution, some individuals' immigration status is unclear. Few would argue that it isn't a source of considerable national embarrassment.

Yet, despite these attitudes, Sam Li was one of the many who came to Britain with ambition and a positive outlook to match. And when circumstances conspired to place him at the very centre of one of the most expansive periods in music history, he seized the opportunity to leave his imprint on the world. And he did so in a manner which few who met him will forget.

Today, Sam Li's work is in the hands of guitar players, enthusiasts and close family. His repairs and refinish jobs have endured and the integrity of his guitar construction was robust enough to survive for decades. All of this should be a lesson: something made with care, pride and attention to detail will last many lifetimes.

'When yuh dead yuh nah sabee, and when yuh sabee yuh dead'
(You spend a lifetime trying to acquire knowledge and understanding and, when it seems that all has been grasped, life ends.)

What is perhaps most touching is that, even in his latter years, Sam Li still had such an incredible appetite for life. Despite frailty and failing health, the sheer joy of being alive, listening to music and spending time with his loved ones, was undiminished.

Fiona Beattie: *One of the last things Sam said to me was that he wanted to live forever.*

Like every human being, Sam Li couldn't live forever. However, his work and his legacy just might…

ACKNOWLEGEMENTS

A chance glimpse of a Pink Floyd poster on a garage wall led to conversations that took me back to the 1970s when my stepfather was a guitar repairer in London.

Until then, I had given no real thought to Sam's work in the music industry, as it was nothing unusual from the family perspective. Those conversations, however, enabled me to see Sam's role with fresh eyes and it was at that point that I felt inspired to do something in his memory.

Having since spoken to musicians of their recollections of Sam, it began to dawn on me that this wasn't simply Sam's story but a piece of history and I was most fortunate to be offered the name of Mark Eglinton, an author with a background in music, to help take Sam's story forward.

My sincere and heartfelt thanks go to all those - too many to name individually - who so very kindly gave their valuable time and provided information or shared their recollections in order to tell this story.

I would also like to thank all those who have worked on producing the book especially Karen Butler of Rudling House, Jake Tynan and of course Mark Eglinton.

This book is dedicated to Sam and is my way of saying thank you to the man who brought me up as his daughter.

Fiona Beattie

MARK EGLINTON

Mark Eglinton is a Scottish bestselling co-writer of several books across multiple genres including Blindsided with Australian rugby legend Michael Lynagh, which was shortlisted for International Autobiography Of The Year at the 2016 British Sports Book Awards and Heavy Duty, KK Downing. Mark is also the co-author of the recently published Michael Owen's book, Reboot.

FIONA BEATTIE

Fiona Beattie grew up in London surrounded by music, with her stepfather playing jazz guitar and her mother playing classical piano. Deciding on a career in technology and after a spell at a Merchant Bank, Fiona furthered her career at the Reuters News Agency. Fiona recently stepped back from technology to dedicate more of her time to her passion of music where she researched the life of her stepfather, his work, the world he inhabited and the larger than life personalities that relied on his craftsmanship. The Guitar Man is the result of this work. Fiona is delighted to have collaborated with the best-selling author Mark Eglinton.